Waterside Walks in
HAMPSHIRE

Nick Battle & Peter Carne

COUNTRYSIDE BOOKS
NEWBURY BERKSHIRE

First published 1997
Reprinted 1998, 1999, 2002, 2008, 2021
New edition published 2016, 2023
© Nicholas Battle 2023

All rights reserved. No part of this publication may be reproduced, stored in a retrieval system, or transmitted by any means, electronic, mechanical, photocopying, recording or otherwise, without the prior written permission of the copyright holder and publishers.

COUNTRYSIDE BOOKS
3 Catherine Road
Newbury, Berkshire

To view our complete range of books please visit us at
www.countrysidebooks.co.uk

ISBN 978 1 84674 339 9

All materials used in the manufacture of this book carry FSC certification.

Produced through The Letterworks Ltd., Reading
Designed and Typeset by KT Designs, St Helens
Printed by Holywell Press, Oxford

Contents

	Introduction	5
	Area map	6

WALKS

1	Stockbridge & Marshcourt River (*2 miles*)	7
2	Bishopstoke & the River Itchen (*5 miles*)	12
3	Shawford & the Itchen Valley (*2 miles*)	17
4	Ovington & Itchen Stoke (*1½ miles*)	00
5	Alresford & the River Alre (*3¾ miles*)	26
6	Romsey & the Andover Canal (*3¼ miles*)	30
7	Wherwell & the Test Way (*3 miles*)	35
8	Barton Stacey & the River Dever (*4¼ miles*)	00
9	The Test at Whitchurch & Laverstoke (*5¾ miles*)	44
10	Micheldever & the Dever Valley (*3½ miles*)	48
11	Dogmersfield & the Basingstoke Canal (*3¼ miles*)	52
12	Froyle & the Wey Valley (*5 miles*)	57
13	Droxford & the River Meon (*2¼ miles*)	61
14	Wallington's River Estuary (*4¼ miles*)	65

Contents (continued)

15	Titchfield & the Lower Meon Valley (5¼ *miles*)	69
16	Bursledon & the Hamble Estuary (4¾ *miles*)	73
17	Calshot & Southampton Water (4¼ *miles*)	77
18	Buckler's Hard & the Beaulieu River (4½ *miles*)	82
19	Pennington & the Solent Shore (3 *miles*)	87
20	Ringwood & the Avon Valley Path (4¾ *miles*)	92

INTRODUCTION

Peter Carne was a great walking enthusiast and this book of walks beside Hampshire's many waterways, when it first appeared, was immediately popular with those who wanted to explore the great river valleys of the county for themselves.

Peter chose his routes carefully. The circular walks all left the waterside for at least a part of the way to give those who followed them the chance to sample some of the neighbouring countryside.

Re-walking the routes has been a really satisfying task. However, I have been most generously helped by a strong team of local walkers to whom I owe special thanks for their dedication and attention to detail. In particular I must single out Vicky Fletcher, Tim Kermode, Rory Batho, Bella Battle, and Jessica and Emily Batho who all had to confront the amendments to rights of way, and all too often the need to turn out in poor weather.

This brings me to some notes for those using the book. Be aware of the countryside that you pass through and the need to respect its code. In particular, keep dogs on a lead if you are in a field with other animals. Cows will generally take little notice of passing walkers unless they feel threatened.

Finally, footwear. Even on the sunniest and driest day you are going to find a muddy patch or two. Bear this in mind, and always wear waterproof walking shoes or boots when you set off into the countryside.

We hope you enjoy these walks beside Hampshire's magnificent rivers.

Nick Battle

Waterside Walks in Hampshire

PUBLISHER'S NOTE

We hope that you obtain considerable enjoyment from this book; great care has been taken in its preparation. Although at the time of publication all routes followed public rights of way or permitted paths, diversion orders can be made and permissions withdrawn.

We cannot, of course, be held responsible for such diversion orders or any inaccuracies in the text which result from these or any other changes to the routes, nor any damage which might result from walkers trespassing on private property. We are anxious, though, that all the details covering the walks are kept up to date, and would therefore welcome information from readers which would be relevant to future editions.

The simple sketch maps that accompany the walks in this book are based on notes made by the author whilst surveying the routes on the ground. They are designed to show you how to reach the start and to point out the main features of the overall circuit, and they contain a progression of numbers that relate to the paragraphs of the text.

However, for the benefit of a proper map, we do recommend that you purchase the relevant Ordnance Survey map covering your walk. Ordnance Survey maps are widely available, especially through booksellers and local newsagents.

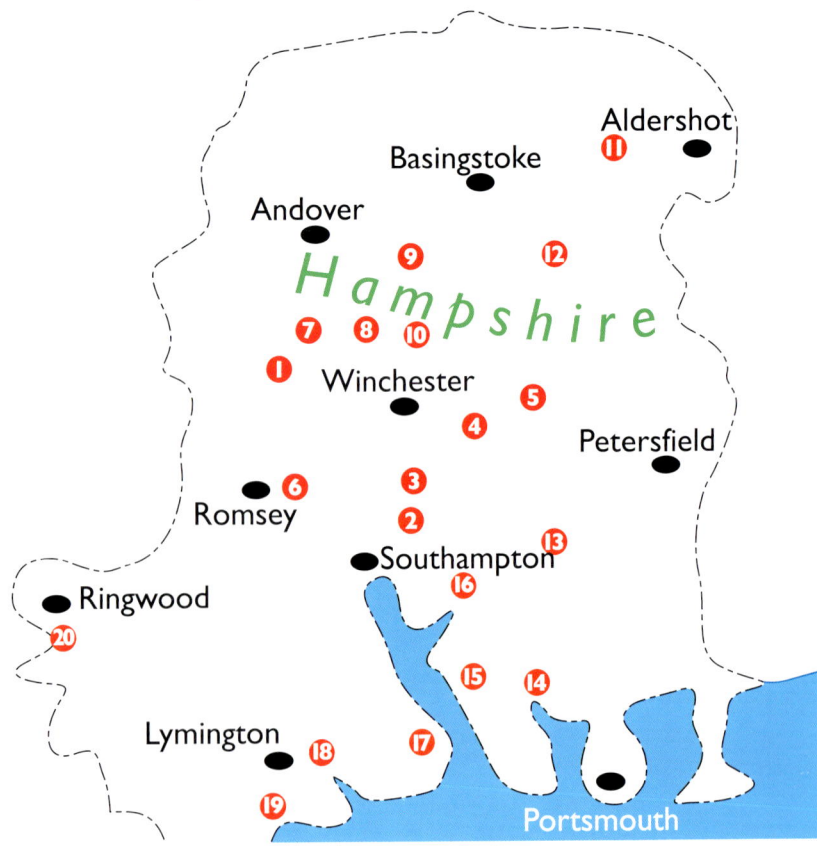

Area Map showing locations of the walks

Stockbridge High Street

Walk 1
STOCKBRIDGE & MARSHCOURT RIVER
2 miles (3.5 km)

Start: Lion's Den Car Park, Cow Drove Hill, Stockbridge, SO20 6JA.
Parking: The main car park for Stockbridge Common.
OS Map: Explorer 131 Romsey, Andover & Test Valley.
Grid Ref: SU357346.
Terrain: Riverside and flat woodland paths. Dog friendly.

This walk explores Marshcourt River, a clear chalk stream which runs parallel with the River Test before merging with it to the south of the town, and Stockbridge Common, owned by the National Trust. Initially you head along the Test Way then amble round the common along a stretch of Marshcourt River to reach the attractive town itself. In the 19th century Stockbridge was a famous horseracing centre with nine racing stables at its peak. A frequent visitor was

Waterside Walks in Hampshire

the Prince of Wales (later Edward VII), who rented two properties in the town, one for himself and the other for Lillie Langtry.

THE WHITE HART is an award-winning 16th-century inn with seating both inside and out. Popular with locals and visitors alike, this Fuller's pub offers a warm welcome and a good menu. ☎ 01264 810663. Alternatively, there are a number of excellent cafés and a deli on the High Street.

The Walk

❶ Head to the rear of the car park, through a gate and turn left on a broad fenced path, the Test Way. *This part of the Test Way follows what was originally an 18th-century canal between Andover and Redbridge near Southampton and was then converted into a railway line. The Sprat and Winkle line, which opened in 1865, had a lot of passenger traffic with race-goers travelling to Stockbridge and troops heading from Salisbury Plain to Southampton and over to France*

Stockbridge Common

Stockbridge & Marshcourt River 1

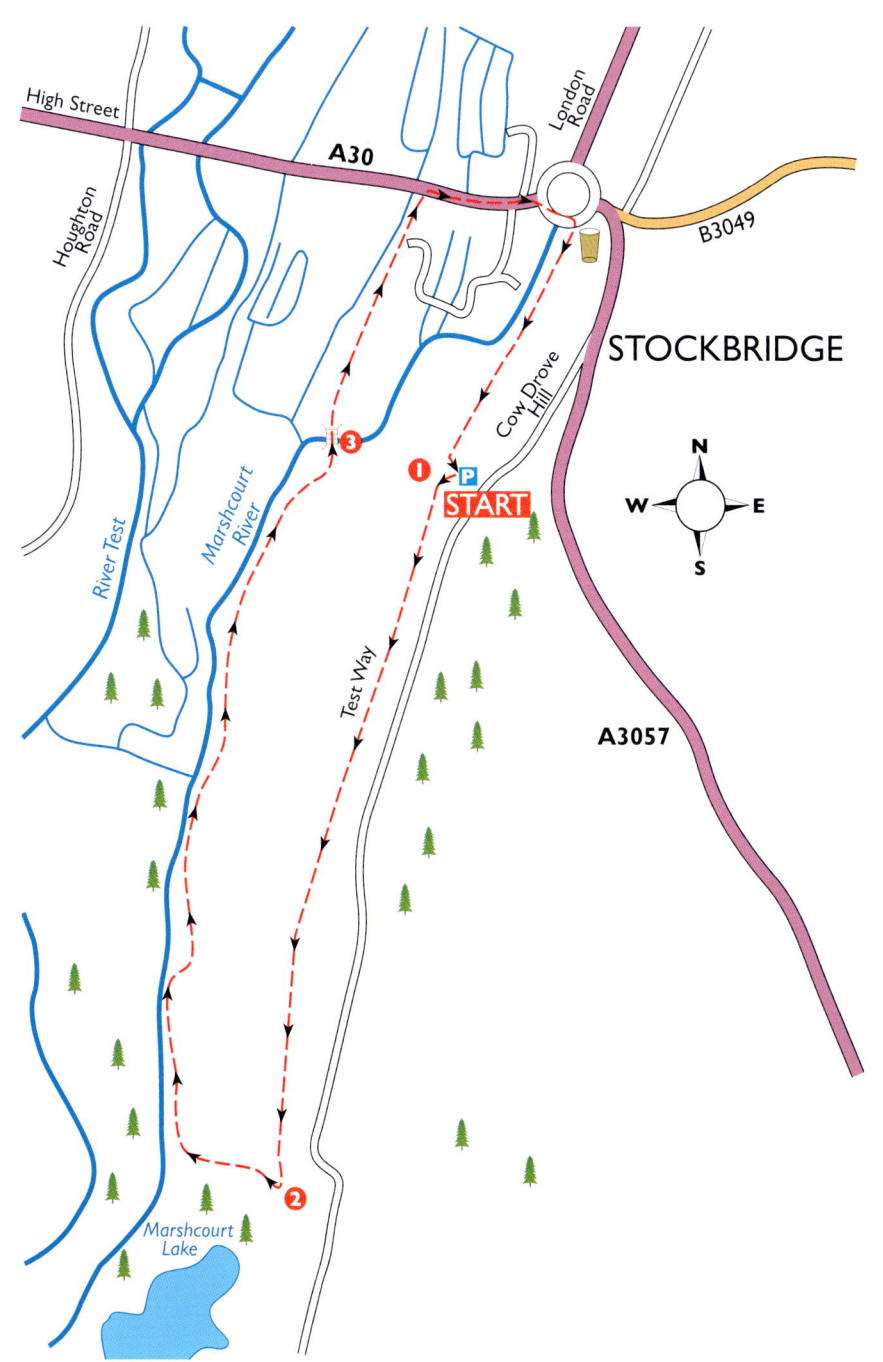

Waterside Walks in Hampshire

during the First and Second World Wars. Stockbridge Station was where the roundabout is now but it closed in 1965 under the Beeching axe. Ignore a gate on the right opposite a path on the left and continue to a second gate on the right, just before the start of a wood on the right. *The large house on the hill to the left is Marshcourt, also spelled Marsh Court, built between 1901 and 1904 by Edward Lutyens. Now privately owned the house was a military hospital during the First World War and was briefly a school in the 1930s.*

❷ Turn right through the gate and go ahead across the common to the river.

At the river, turn right and walk along this attractive stretch of the Marshcourt River until you reach a narrow bridge.

❸ Cross the bridge and continue ahead across a field and then beside a branch of the river to emerge on Stockbridge High Street. Here you will find a number of independent cafés and shops that are worth exploring. To continue the walk turn right and head to a roundabout. Turn right along Trafalgar Way just before the White Hart pub. At the end of the road continue ahead along the Test Way to return to the car park.

The Test Way

Walk 2
BISHOPSTOKE & THE RIVER ITCHEN
5 miles (8 km)

Start: The Hub, Bishopstoke Road, Eastleigh, SO50 6LA.
Parking: Pay and display car park at the Hub leisure centre.
OS Map: Outdoor Leisure 22 New Forest. **Grid Ref:** SU463192.
Terrain: Riverside paths and flat grassy meadows with a short steep climb through woodland. Dog friendly.

Waterside walkers are spoilt for choice along the peaceful Itchen Valley and you'll be glad not to have missed this part of it from the very moment you set off. Follow a splendid path alongside the old Itchen Navigation, then return over wide meadows close to the river itself.

Waterside Walks in Hampshire

STEAM TOWN BREW CO combines a taproom and burger bar and is on Bishopstoke Road towards Eastleigh. The name is a nod to Eastleigh's industrial railway heritage and extends to much of the décor. The food and service are both excellent. ☎ 02382 359139. Another option is the **BAMBRIDGE PARK GARDEN CENTRE**, about half-way along this walk, which has a café. ☎ 01962 713707.

The Walk

1 Go through the gate in the corner of the car park, opposite the Hub. This leads directly to the path along the Itchen Navigation, where you turn left to follow the river. This is part of the Itchen Way. Ignore a path which soon turns right to bridge the canal. Keep the canal on your right as you head north, at first with playing fields to your left, followed by meadows as you carry on through quiet countryside. Your path becomes gravelled and bridges side streams more than once. In around ¾ mile you reach Withymead Lock where you cross the Navigation on a metal footbridge to the tree-shaded east bank, which you now follow, presently veering slightly left to pass under the London-Southampton railway by a rather low brick arch.

2 Back gardens slope down to the waterway on your left as your path follows it along a right-hand curve, before once again passing under the railway. A few metres further on you reach and cross the busy B3335 with care, and then continue north past a triple weir, with the Navigation still on your left. In ¾ mile, a river channel flanks your path on the right, and you continue with water flowing on both sides – and sometimes through culverts beneath your path – until you emerge onto Kiln Lane.

3 Turn right and walk along the road to a bridge over the Itchen. Through trees on your left you can catch a glimpse of Brambridge House, once the home of Mrs Fitzherbert whom George IV secretly married, although the union was never officially recognised. After the bridge you come to the entrance to Brambridge Park Garden Centre, which is a good place to stop for a break. Continue a little further along the main road passing Bridge Cottage then turn right through a small gateway to a kissing gate, also on your right. Follow this signposted footpath parallel with the right-hand edge of the meadow you now enter. Pass through a kissing gate at the end of this meadow and then two further kissing gates through

Bishopstoke & the River Itchen 2

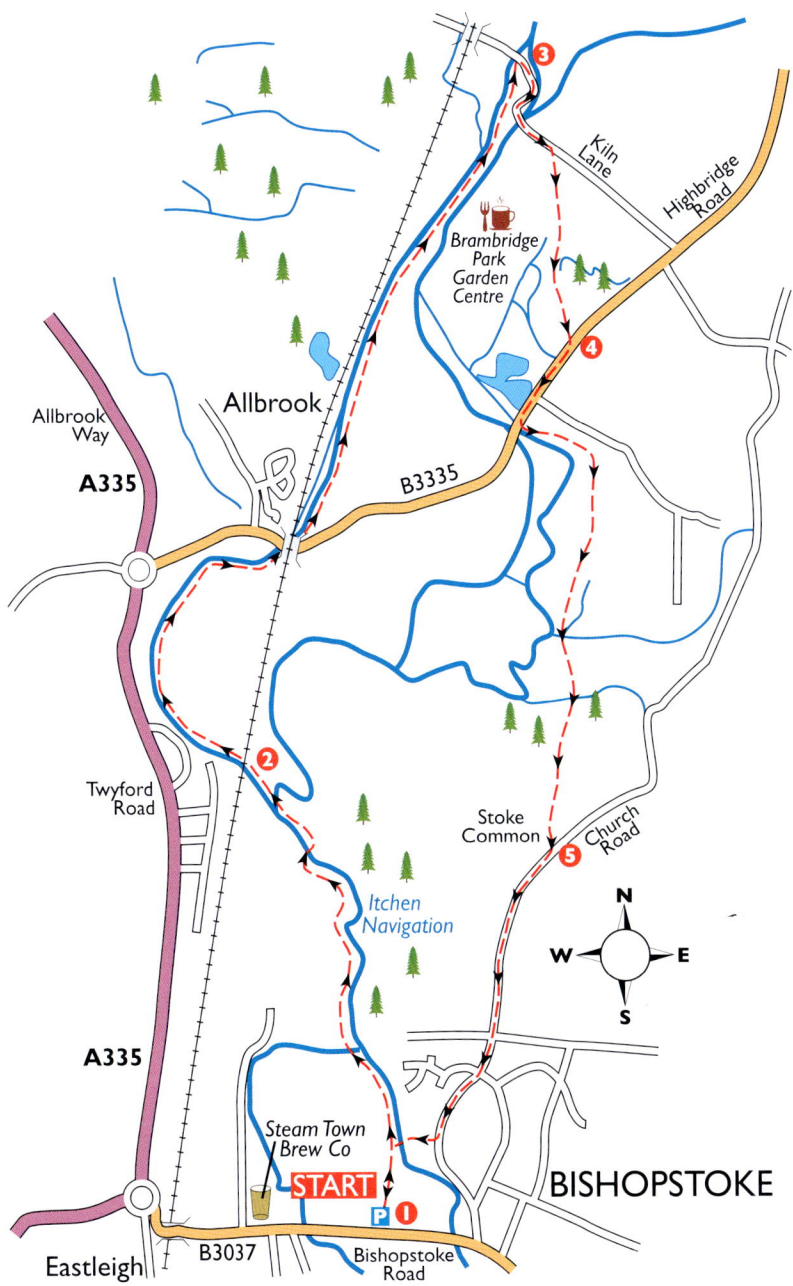

Bishopstoke & the River Itchen

woodland and into a third meadow. Halfway along the far left edge a stile brings you back onto the B3335.

4 Cross this and follow it to the right past some cottages to the near side of a bridge. Turn left here to follow a footpath with the back gardens of houses to your left. After crossing a kissing gate this joins another path which soon becomes an unfenced grassy track which you follow, slightly to the right across a large pasture flanked by woodland away to your left and straight ahead. Beyond a gap in a straggly hedge the grassy track continues and you follow it to the meadow's end, where a kissing gate leads to a footbridge over a stream before a further meadow. Head for the gate on the far side and another stream footbridge marks the start of a rising woodland path which at first angles slightly right and then is stepped at steeper points. A fence on the left flanks the final stretch of this path, which at Stoke Common joins a road.

5 Turn right and follow Church Road for about ½ mile, past the flint church of St Mary until you come to Oakbank Road on your right. Follow this to a tarmac path through trees and alongside the Itchen Navigation. Cross a bridge and turn left to follow the path back to the car park which you soon reach on your right.

15

Walk 3

SHAWFORD & THE ITCHEN VALLEY

2 miles (3.2 km)

Start: The Bridge Inn, 2 The Stables, Shawford, SO21 2BP.

Parking: There is a large pay and display car park behind the Bridge Inn, and a public car park at the foot of Shawford Down. There is also some limited roadside parking.

OS Map: Explorer 132 Winchester. **Grid Ref:** SU475250.

Terrain: Mostly flat riverside paths with some stretches across uneven meadows. Dog friendly.

This short but unforgettable walk covers part of the Itchen Valley where the chalk which cradles the river crowds in quite closely on both sides. Its proximity emphasises the smooth, green sweep of the river which holds your gaze as

Shawford & the Itchen Valley

it passes you. The river proper shares its water with the Itchen Navigation, here in full flow where it bounds the garden of the Bridge Inn at Shawford, as happily situated a pub for waterside walkers as could be wished for.

THE BRIDGE INN, owned by Chef & Brewer, is a white-fronted pub alongside the Itchen Navigation. There is a seasonal menu served in the large garden where there is plenty of seating or, on colder days you can choose to sit in the cosy bar near the fire. ☎ 01962 713171. Alternatively, try **PLATFORM 1**, just by the railway station, where you'll find a coffee house and gelato.

The Walk

❶ Leaving the Bridge Inn behind you on your left, cross the first bridge, over the Itchen Navigation, and then immediately turn left to follow a hard path north along the Navigation's tree-shaded bank. Soon a footbridge takes you across a side stream leading to Shawford's old mill on your right. Your path continues alongside the Navigation, flanked on its far side by the gardens of a series of fairly large houses. This is also part of the Itchen Way. Path-side trees partly screen your view across water meadows to your right.

❷ Just before reaching another footbridge —with the remains of an old Navigation lock just beyond it, turn right to go through a kissing gate and over a footbridge. Turn slightly left and head along the boardwalk to the field-gate ahead to where a cattle bridge over another river channel precedes a gateway. The footpath ahead follows the right-hand edge of further pasture to another field-gate at its far right corner. Follow the track ahead, soon bridging a main arm of the Itchen by an old mill to your right. Your track then climbs to the main Winchester to Botley road.

17

Waterside Walks in Hampshire

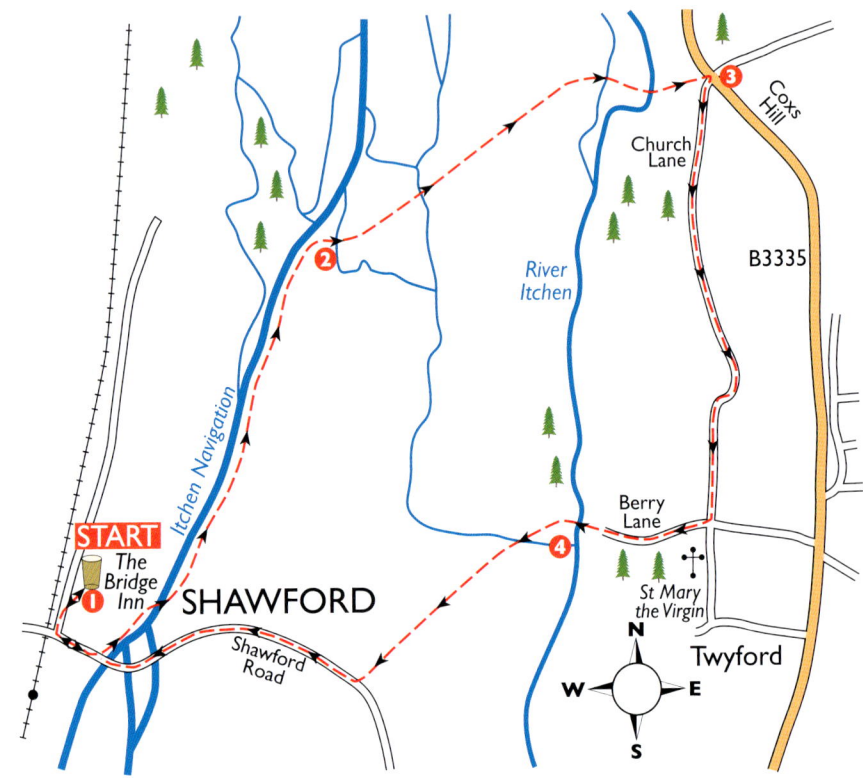

❸ At the road (Coxs Hill), immediately bear right from it to follow Church Lane, which you follow until you reach Twyford's church of St Mary the Virgin. *There has been a church on this site since Saxon times, and before that there may have been a Druidic temple, twelve Druid stones having been found under the tower of the Norman church demolished in 1876 to make way for the present building. The large yew tree in the churchyard may not be quite 1,000 years old, as some have claimed, but it is beyond doubt a very ancient and splendid specimen of its kind.* At the churchyard turn right to follow a downhill track to a footbridge by a cattle bridge over a main stream of the Itchen. Cross this and a kissing gate to enter a meadow where, after a few metres, two separate footpaths diverge.

❹ Take the path on the left to go over a footbridge and then bear right to cross the meadow. When you reach the far side of this pasture your path bends

Shawford & the Itchen Valley 3

left to reach Shawford Road. Cross over the road to the pavement and turn right passing the grounds of Shawford Park mansion on your left. Cross a bridge over a side-channel of the Itchen by Shawford's old mill on your right and then soon re-cross the Navigation to the Bridge Inn and your walk's end. If time and energy permit, extend your walk west to enjoy a brief and bracing climb of Shawford Down, a county-owned open space from the top of which the Itchen Valley presents a truly spectacular panoramic view.

Tim Kermode

Walk 4
Ovington & Itchen Stoke
1½ miles (2.4 km)

Start: The Bush Inn, Ovington, SO24 0RE.
Parking: Park at the Bush Inn, with permission from the landlord. There is also some parking space on the approach road.
OS Map: Explorer 132 Winchester. **Grid Ref:** SU562318.
Terrain: Mostly flat riverside footpaths with some road walking along a pavement or very quiet lanes. Dog friendly.

Approached by narrow, tree-lined lanes and well hidden from the world outside until you actually arrive there, Ovington's recorded history stretches back to the time when land here was granted by King Edgar to the Bishop of Winchester. Of Anglo-Saxon origin, its name means 'a place above' and might equally

Ovington & Itchen Stoke 4

imply 'a place apart' from the bustle of modern life, so steeped in calm does it remain. Clustering cottages and farm buildings are overlooked by a 19th-century church dedicated to St Peter. Just to the north of the present steepled building stood its Norman predecessor, of which the entrance arch is all that has been preserved.

THE BUSH INN is a popular riverside pub with an attractive garden. Tradition has it that this was a stopping place for pilgrims en route to Canterbury, although how they can ever have found it seems today a matter of mystery. So well secluded is it that few modern travellers can claim to have discovered it purely by chance. Yet people come here from all over Hampshire and well beyond, attracted by its reputation. The Bush makes the perfect start for this short but lovely walk. ☎ 01962 732764.

The Walk

1 With the Bush Inn behind you on your left, follow the lane for a few metres before turning left to follow a footpath through bushes and across the River Itchen by a footbridge. The glorious river views here almost always include waterbirds, with

Waterside Walks in Hampshire

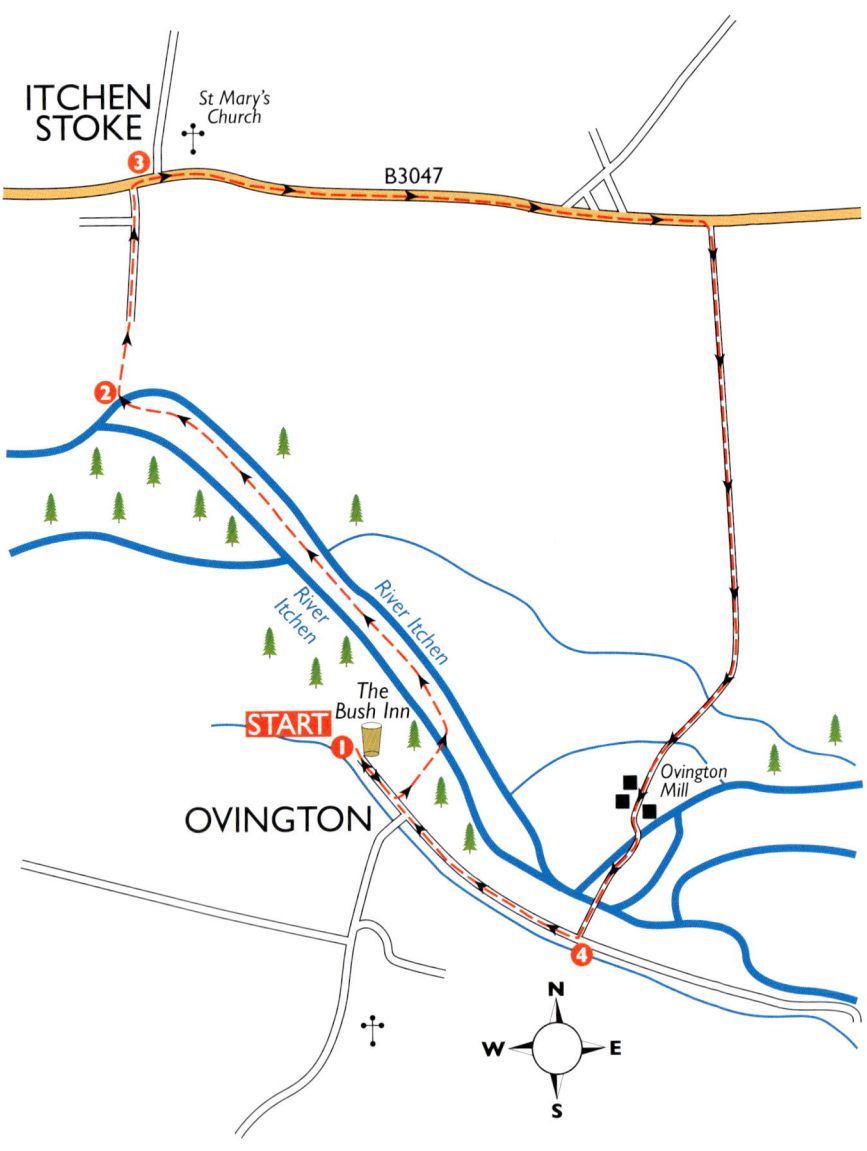

swans, wild ducks, coots and moorhens to admire. Continue left as the path turns in that direction, now with the main river to your left and a minor side-channel to your right. The waterside section of this walk and the lane from the river to Itchen Stoke follows part of the Itchen Way. A steadily

Ovington & Itchen Stoke 4

widening swathe of trees develops between you and the main river as you head west, but the right-hand channel remains alongside you all the way to where your path bridges it close to its confluence with the main channel.

2 Cross the bridge and follow a lane away from the river flanked by trees and by Itchen Stoke's cottages. Turn right alongside a thatched dwelling which was once the village schoolhouse. *Just across the road, on your left, is the parish church of St Mary, an imposing, elevated, spireless structure based in design on a parish chapel. It was built in 1866 at the expense of the then vicar, but closed just over a century later, and is now being looked after by the Fund for Redundant Churches, though occasional services are still held.*

St Mary's Church, Itchen Stoke

Waterside Walks in Hampshire

❸ Continue along a paved roadside path for ¼ mile. From here you can enjoy a southerly view across the lush, tree-bordered pastures of this peaceful stretch of the Itchen Valley. Where the path ends, turn right to follow a narrow downhill lane between trees to a watersplash flanked by a footbridge. A left-ward twist of the lane passes Ovington Mill and bridges its millrace before crossing the main river.

❹ You now turn right at a T-junction to head back west with the broad sweep of the Itchen's main stream to your right and a minor channel to your left at the foot of a steep, timbered bank. The Bush Inn lies just ahead, on your right.

Ovington Mill

Walk 5
ALRESFORD & THE RIVER ALRE

3¾ miles (6 km)

Start: Alresford Railway Station, Station Road, Alresford, SO24 9JG.
Parking: Alresford Station pay and display car park just off Station Road.
OS Map: Explorer 132 Winchester. **Grid Ref:** SU588325.
Terrain: Good riverside and grassy field paths with some road walking along mostly quiet lanes. Dog friendly.

The little town of New Alresford was planned and developed 800 years ago as a centre for rural commerce. Broad Street, at its centre, dates from that period and was made deliberately wide to accommodate sheep fairs and other trade gatherings. At around the same time a high

Waterside Walks in Hampshire

embankment was constructed across the oddly-named River Alre, one of several chalk streams that come together in this area of mid-Hampshire to create the River Itchen. A very large lake was formed, the shrunken remnant of which survives as Old Alresford Pond. The man behind all this was a Winchester bishop, Godfrey de Lucy, who had a palace at nearby Bishop's Sutton, the supply of fresh fish for which was almost certainly the prime purpose of the great pond!

A duck-thronged lake, a lovely old watermill, the River Alre (pron. Ah-rl), and a path which ranks among the county's best for waterside interest and charm. These are yours to see and enjoy on this walk from the 'watercress capital' of Hampshire.

THE GLOBE pub lies in an area called 'The Soke' at the south-western end of Old Alresford Pond, reached at the last stage of our walk. There is a pretty garden to relax in at the back with views across the pond. Ask them to tell you about their annual duck race each June! ☎ 01962 733118.

The Walk

❶ From the station car park, follow Station Road to join the town's main street opposite the Bell Hotel. Turn right for a few metres, then go left into the well-named Broad Street. Keep straight on down Mill Hill lane at the bottom, and in 200 metres turn left along Ladywell Lane, a cul-de-sac with flanking cottages and paths leading to a hard-surfaced footpath with the River Alre to your right.

❷ Keep ahead, passing Alresford Memorial Gardens. The river is then straddled by Alresford's beautiful and picturesque Fulling Mill. *Dating from the 13th century it is now a privately owned house. When the cloth industry established larger mills during the 19th century it became derelict but was saved and converted into a private residence in the 1950s.* Your path continues along the riverside path, and eventually swings right past the end of a road called The Dean and into increasingly rural surroundings, with trees overhanging the water. Soon you bridge the Alre as you skirt the Eel House, an old derelict riverside building. *It dates back to the 1820s when it was constructed to intercept mature European eels as they travelled downstream to their breeding grounds.* With swirling water now on your left, continue to another footbridge over the water to your right. Cross, then your path emerges through trees to join a lane, which you follow ahead, going steadily uphill.

Alresford & the River Alre 5

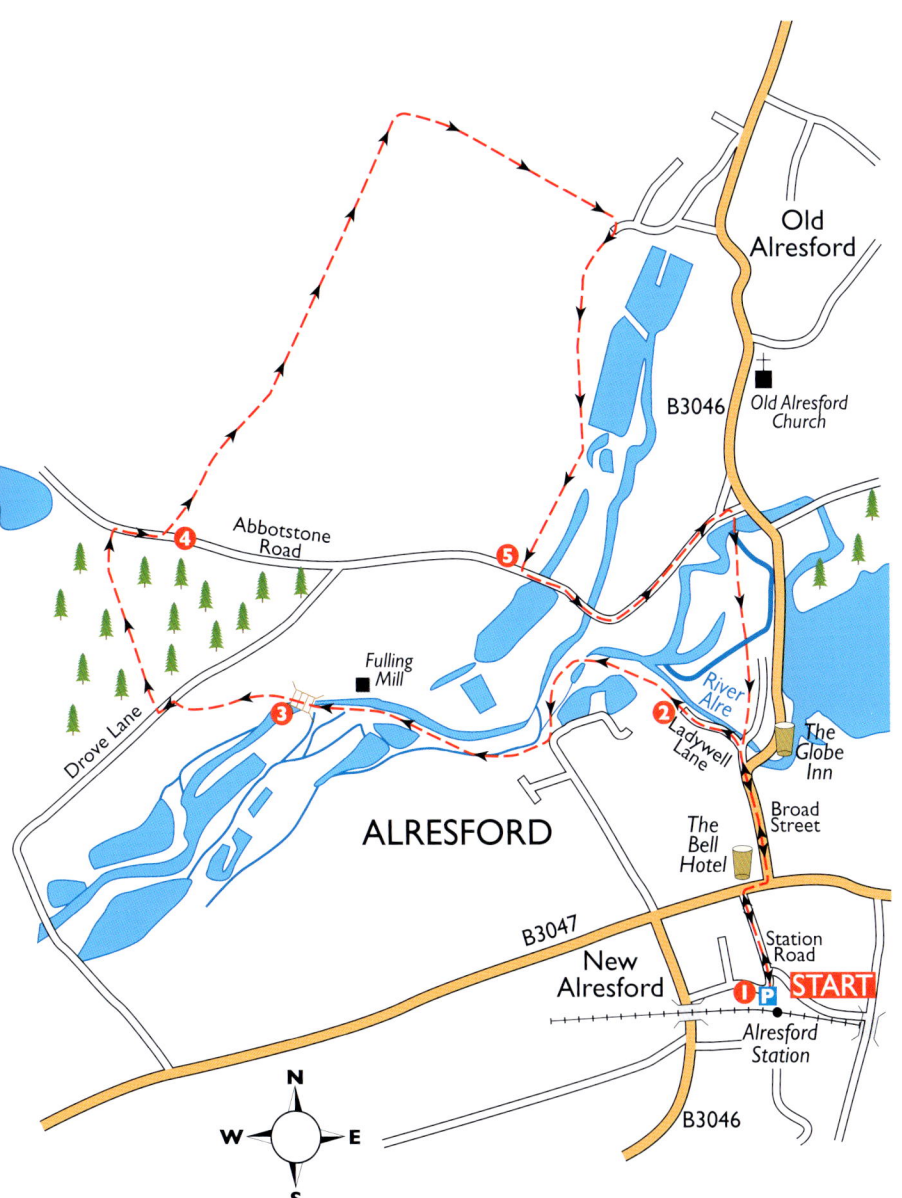

3 The path then levels out and you come to a gate which you pass through and follow a concreted lane going uphill to the right. This then leads to a lane (Drove Lane) which you cross then continue diagonally left, onto a path which leads

Waterside Walks in Hampshire

Watercress beds

through the hedge on the opposite side. Keep right, up the hill, with a vineyard on your left and a hedge on your right. You pass over the peak with fine valley views before dropping down to a further quiet country lane (Abbotstone Road), reached through a kissing gate on the right at the bottom. Turn right onto this lane for a few metres, then turn left along a signposted right of way.

4 Follow the path. In ¼ mile you come to a crossroads of lanes which you pass over. Keep ahead along a narrower path and, in just under ½ mile, you come to another junction where you turn right along another hedged green lane. Follow this going downhill to the right. When you reach the road turn right. Follow this road with a hedge on your left and houses on your right and ignore all side turnings. The path then turns

Alresford & the River Alre

into a grassy path with high hedges at the side. When you reach the point where a yellow footpath sign on the right points to a gate, take this. Beyond it, follow the hedge to your left along farmland with distant views of Old Alresford church up to your left. Pass through a wooden kissing gate and on into the next field. There are now watercress beds on your left. Soon you pass some cottages on the right, then you reach a road (Abbotstone Road), with a flint wall facing you, where you turn left.

5 Cross a small bridge above a clear, small tributary of the Alre, a good place for spotting fish. Soon the road swings left and begins to go gently uphill. Just before you reach the main Basingstoke to Alresford road, by the 30 mph sign, turn right by a wooden fence along a narrow footpath that passes more (disused) watercress beds. Pass Alresford's Town Mill, now converted into apartments, with its spectacular multi-tiered cascade. At the end of the building, turn left and go up some steps to cross a bridge with the river swirling noisily just below your feet. Join the main road opposite the Globe Inn. Continue up into Broad Street, passing the lovely Old Fire Station building with its red door, to return to your car.

Walk 6

ROMSEY & THE ANDOVER CANAL

3¼ miles (5.4 km)

Start: Alma Road Car Park, Alma Road, Romsey, SO51 8ED.

Parking: Park at the pay and display car park off Alma Road.

OS Map: Explorer 131 Romsey, Andover & Test Valley.
Grid Ref: SU355213.

Terrain: Canal towpath and a small amount of road walking along pavement. Dog friendly.

The closing decades of the 18th century saw a frenzy of canal construction in many parts of England. One of the fruits of this was the Andover to Redbridge Canal, locally referred to as the Barge Canal. Some 22 miles long, with 24 locks and a rise of 169 ft from south to north, this followed a parallel

Romsey & the Andover Canal 6

course with the mighty River Test. Sadly, not much is left, the Andover to Redbridge railway was built in part over where it once ran, but this walk explores the main surviving 2-mile stretch, alongside which the former towpath offers a pleasant waterside walk along the wide valley of the River Test.

THE OLD HOUSE AT HOME, on Love Lane just next to the car park, is a thatched 17th-century building with an attractive beer garden at the back. ☎ 01794 513175. Alternatively try award-winning **DISH, DELI AND KITCHEN** on Latimer Street, just before you reach The Hundred. ☎ 01794 513663.

The Walk

❶ From Alma Road car park turn right heading back to Alma Road. Turn right again and cross the road (there are lights at the T-junction ahead for a safer crossing). Turn left at the T-junction which takes you to a roundabout by the beautiful Plaza Theatre; an art deco gem from 1931. Take the turning to the left of the theatre and join the towpath of the old canal, with the canal itself on your right.

❷ After a short distance you will see the railway bridge ahead and, just before it to the right is Romsey Signal Box, a working railway museum. If it is not open when you pass, you could always turn right and have a look through the railings. Returning to the route, go under the railway and continue along the canal-side path for just over a mile. Leaving the houses behind you, the canal remains on your right and Fishlake Meadows Nature Reserve opens up to your left.

❸ You then reach a concrete canal crossing point and a crossroads of paths. To the left is what appears to be an enclosed electricity substation. Beyond it on the left is a high pole carrying electricity. At this crossroads, turn left down onto the path which crosses the broad valley of the Test. Follow this path with a rich array of wild flowers and plants all around you. The path eventually narrows and passes into trees, then almost immediately you go over water along a board walk. *You have just crossed the wide flood plain of the River Test. You can imagine the devastation caused to the local landscape in past centuries when the river flooded. Today it is tamed and controlled. The weed along it is regularly cut and then allowed to flow downstream to a barrier just ½ mile to the north of where you are standing. There it is trapped and a hydraulic grab lifts it*

Waterside Walks in Hampshire

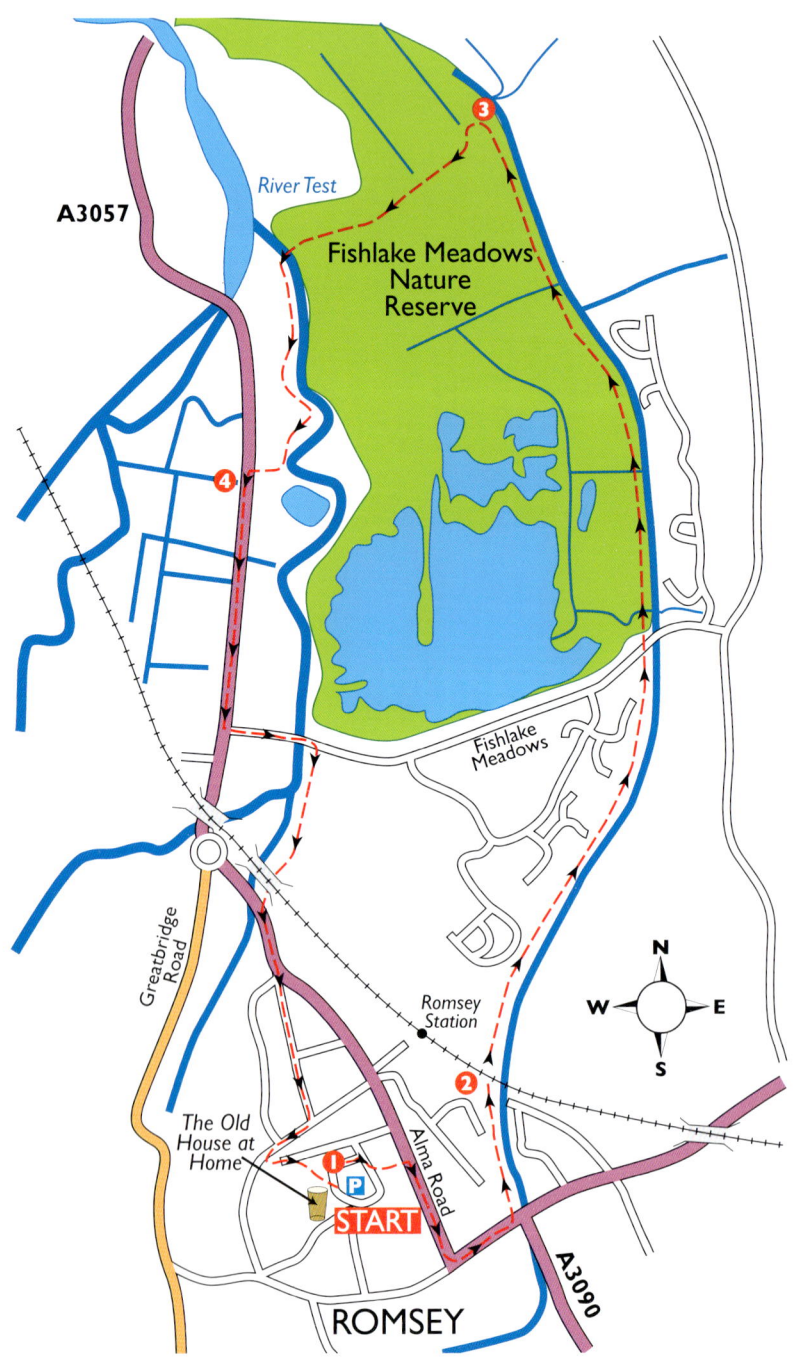

Romsey & the Andover Canal

Waterside Walks in Hampshire

all out onto land for recycling. Continue ahead to where the track emerges at a path beside a tributary of the Test. Turn left and walk along the path with extremely tall trees on your left. A bridge then takes you to the other side of the river. With the river now on your left, follow the path, which ends at a tree-lined avenue, where you turn right to go up to the main road.

❹ Turn left here, where there is a good pavement. When you see the railway bridge ahead of you turn left down Fishlake Meadows road. Cross over the road when it reaches a bridge and after it turn right along a signed footpath. The path passes a sluice and then a huge weeping willow. When you reach another metalled road, cross over it and continue ahead, soon passing underneath the main railway line, to join the main road going back into Romsey. Turn left and when the road swings round to the left keep ahead along Duttons Road until you reach Station Road where you turn right. Turn left into Orchard Lane to return to the car park or keep ahead for the town centre where you will find a good selection of cafés and restaurants.

Chilbolton Cow Common

Walk 7
WHERWELL & THE TEST WAY
3 miles (5 km)

Start: Wherwell Church, Church Street, SP11 7JH.

Parking: There is limited roadside parking in Wherwell. Park at the White Lion Inn if eating or drinking there (with landlord permission), or there is a small car park next to the church.

OS Map: Explorer 131 Romsey, Andover & Test Valley.

Grid Ref: SU389409.

Terrain: No significant gradients, mostly flat tracks and riverside paths. Dog friendly.

Wherwell, with its attractive thatched and timber-framed dwellings, is located alongside a river universally acknowledged as being the queen of English trout streams – indeed, perhaps the most famous trout-fishing water anywhere. Leading from one lovely old village to another via one of the most delightful stretches of the Test Way, then back again over an

Waterside Walks in Hampshire

attractive common, this short ramble twice crosses the River Test at scenic spots where you will want to linger awhile, if only to feed the ducks.

THE WHITE LION INN, in the heart of Wherwell, is a former coaching inn dating from 1611 and offers a warm welcome and varied lunchtime and dinner menus. ☎ 01264 860317. **THE ABBOTS MITRE** in Chilbolton is a popular traditional English pub where the service is good and food is all freshly prepared. ☎ 01264 860348. There is also an excellent tea room opposite **CHILBOLTON VILLAGE SHOP & TEA ROOM.**
☎ 01264 860231.

The Walk

1 From Church Street turn left by the war memorial to reach the White Lion Inn on a corner where the road bends right. With the pub on your left, head uphill and across the road to reach a former railway bridge. *Wherwell station used to be just left of this bridge. There are few traces of it now, although the ticket office, waiting room and Station Master's House have been converted into private dwellings. To the south of Chilbolton parts of the line now form the Test Way.*

After the bridge, look for a narrow footpath between fences on the left, signed for the Test Way (the path is slightly hidden but can be found to the left of the metal gates). Follow the narrow path until you reach the road, where you turn right. On the bend in the road keep left to continue along the Test Way. Follow the left-hand edge of a sloping field where chalky subsoil shows through in places. At the end of the field turn left into the trees and down steps towards the cottages and road below.

2 Turn left back towards the village. After a few metres, turn right following signs for the Test Way onto a long bridge spanning converging channels of the tree-fringed River Test. Continue straight on along the well-worn path across Chilbolton Cow Common, an ancient meadow where cattle sometimes wallow belly deep in the fringing waterways. *Both the common and the River Test are designated as a Site of Special Scientific Interest for nature conservation. The common is especially beautiful in spring and summer with irises, cowslips and orchids to name but a few of the rare flowers which can be seen here.* The path continues to a further river footbridge. Immediately after crossing this turn left, following a river pathway for a matter of metres to a kissing gate. Follow the pathway

Wherwell & the Test Way 7

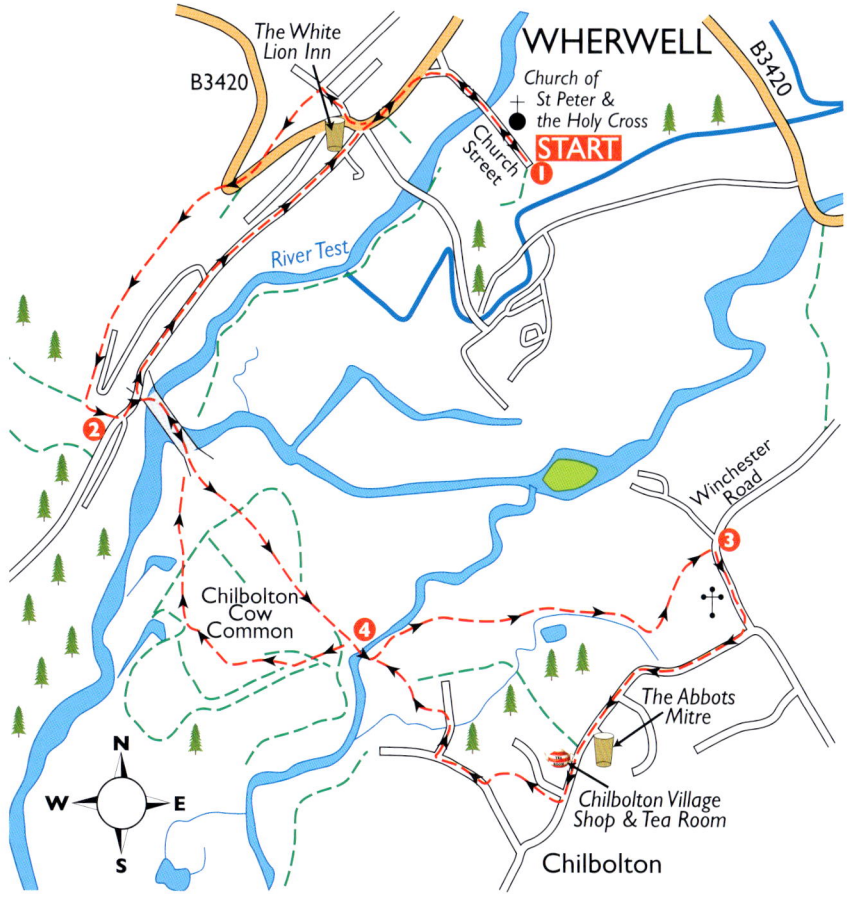

between hedges to the back of two thatched cottages and a further kissing gate, then continue straight on through a third kissing gate. Follow the path beside a small stream where you can see the church to the left across the fields. Turn left through a fourth kissing gate and through a field. The path now leads around the church and up to a road (Winchester Road). If you wish to visit the church, turn right and enter the churchyard here.

Local flint and chalk and some Isle of Wight stone went into the construction some 800 years ago of the small village church of St Mary-the-Less. Exactly which St Mary the church is dedicated to is uncertain, but the 'Less' name refers to a lesser or younger church than a senior or parent church that existed prior to the Dissolution, under Henry VIII.

❸ Turn right along Winchester Road to reach a junction of roads. You are now at the eastern end of Chilbolton, a Test Valley village equally filled with old-world charm as its neighbour, Wherwell. Turn right into the village, enjoying the thatched cottages and past the Abbots Mitre and Chilbolton Village Shop & Tea Room, both also thatched. A few metres past the shop look out for a footpath sign on the right, opposite Upcote Cottage. Follow this hedged path between gardens, and bending left to join Joy's Lane. Turn right into the lane back towards Chilbolton Cow Common, over a cattle grid and into a public car park. The track divides here; bear right towards some cottages, and after a few metres turn left across the common (signposted Test Way), and back towards the bridge which you re-cross.

❹ Bear left to skirt the left-hand edge of the common, circling clockwise to follow the main river back to rejoin the Test Way path. Turn left, and head back across the long bridge into Wherwell. Reaching the road, follow this right to Church Street and back to your car.

38

Walk 8
Barton Stacey & the River Dever
4¼ miles (6.8 km)

Start: Barton Stacey Recreation Ground Car Park, Newton Lane, Barton Stacey, SO21 3RP.

Parking: Park in the village car park signposted from the church opposite the playing fields. Walkers using The Swan Inn may leave their cars in the pub's rear car park.

OS Map: Explorer 144 Basingstoke. **Grid Ref:** SU433411.

Terrain: Mostly flat grassy paths and quiet lanes with a couple of stiles but all are dog friendly. Can be very wet underfoot in parts, even on dry days.

Sample the charms of this clear chalk trout river from the lanes and paths which pass alongside it for much of this route. The walk starts in the pretty village of Barton Stacey where nearly all of its cottages were thatched until a devastating fire swept through it in 1792. All Saints church

Waterside Walks in Hampshire

was luckily spared and has been the centre of the community for nearly 1,000 years. In the early part of the 20th century, much of the Barton Stacey estate was allowed to fall into disrepair by its owner to avoid taxes and it became known as a derelict village. The estates were requisitioned in the Second World War for use as a military training area, and former Ministry of Defence army homes still remain in the village, standing slightly apart from the older houses.

THE SWAN INN, a former coaching inn, lies at the heart of the village. This is a friendly country pub where traditional ales, good food and a warm welcome can be counted on. ☎ 01962 760470. There is also **BARTON STACEY STORES,** next to the pub, if you are just wanting a snack or drink.

The Walk

❶ Turn left out of the car park towards the church. When you reach the main village road turn left, and then left again immediately past the churchyard to follow a grassy, downhill track to a kissing gate. The footpath leads you diagonally right across a paddock to a second kissing gate. Head straight across the next field to a further kissing gate, the path then crosses to a footbridge over a stream, beyond which you emerge onto a narrow, little-used lane. Turn right along this lane, soon passing an ancient chalk-rubble 'cob' wall to your

Barton Stacey & the River Dever 8

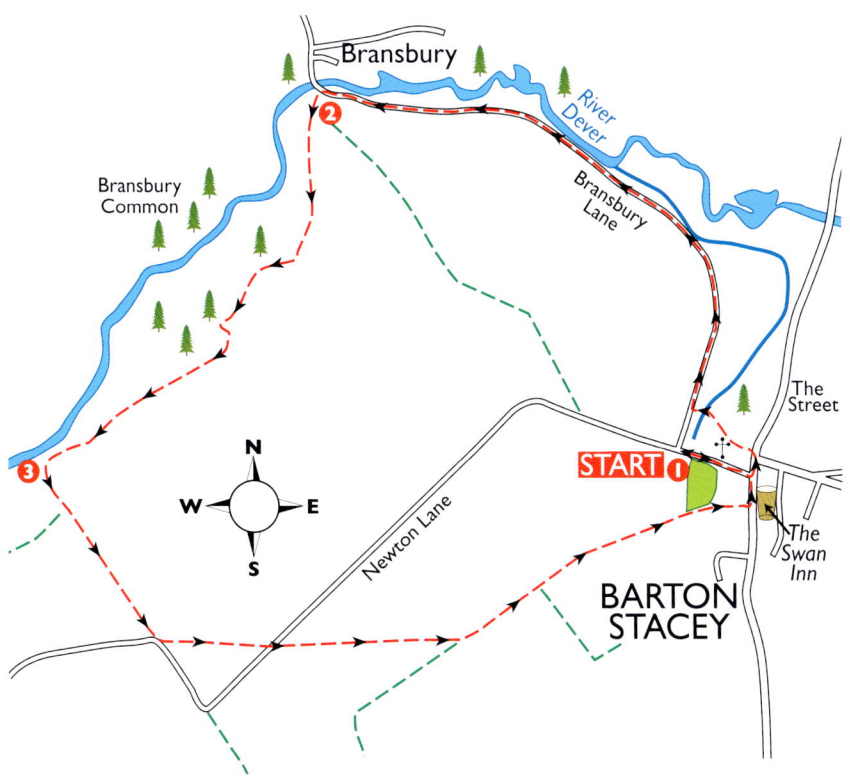

right topped with traditional thatch coping, an uncommon sight these days. After a brief ascent the lane heads steadily downhill, with water in view in the Dever Valley to your right. Soon you find yourself walking parallel with the rippling River Dever, partly screened from your view at first by trees. As you head west the river draws closer, with a millrace alongside you and then the mill, now a private residence.

2 River and lane stay close together as far as a bridge over the Dever, where the lane turns sharply right for the hamlet of Bransbury, just ahead. Do not cross the bridge, instead turn left to follow a hedged track. Ignore the restricted byway signposted off to the left, continuing straight on along the meandering bridleway flanked by farmland on your left and a long stretch of scrub woodland on your right. Where the woodland ends you emerge onto Bransbury Common (open access land), a Site of Special Scientific Interest. This broad and bushy riverside

pasture lies at the point where the River Dever meets the Test. Keep to the higher ground to avoid getting wet feet. The path becomes ill-defined in places but keep as close to the common's leftward edge as conditions permit and you will fairly soon see the River Dever sweeping into view. The River Test flows on the far side of the common, with Herewood Forest visible in the distance. Here the fence on your left-hand side bends left, and you also turn in that direction.

3 Pass through a gate to follow a tree-bordered track which was once a Roman road and is now a public path. A little way along, disregard a track which turns right and continue straight on along the restricted byway until the track you are following joins a road (Newton Lane). Immediately on your left cross over a stile following a footpath sign diagonally left across arable farmland, cutting across the corner of the field to a second stile and rejoining Newton Lane within a few hundred metres. Cross the road following the footpath signs in line with the path just followed, and over another two stiles. Climb gently to cross a low ridge of arable chalkland which is sometimes barred to public access when a red flag warns that the Chilbolton firing range is in use – in which case stay on the road and turn left back to Barton Stacey. Otherwise, follow the footpath over the rise of the hill and downhill to where it joins a farm track flanked by a hedgerow. Turn left and keep the field boundary on your right-hand side. After bridging a stream follow the right-hand edge of a playing field and up a track to rejoin the main village road in Barton Stacey. Turn left and follow the road past the Swan Inn. If you have parked in the village car park, keep on past the pub and turn left just before the church to rejoin Newton Lane and the recreational ground.

Whitchurch Silk Mill

Walk 9
THE TEST AT WHITCHURCH & LAVERSTOKE

5¾ miles (9 km)

Start: Whitchurch Silk Mill, Winchester Street, RG28 7AJ.

Parking: There is a free public car park next to Whitchurch Silk Mill, off Church Street. Roadside parking is also available.

OS Map: Explorer 144 Basingstoke. **Grid Ref:** SU463479.

Terrain: Wooded slopes, parkland, wide green fields and riverside paths. Dog friendly.

Whitchurch preserves the atmosphere of an old country town and is famous for its celebrated silk mill, where robes and gowns for legal luminaries and others have long been made.

Enjoy the upper reaches of the famous River Test and the scenic valley through which it winds at their incomparable best on this walk from the

Waterside Walks in Hampshire

old north Hampshire town. Wooded slopes, parkland trees and wide green fields enfold the river; while overlooking the valley from both sides is rolling chalkland. You'll head out towards the small village of Laverstoke, passing Freefolk's 13th-century church before returning to Whitchurch where a visit to the silk mill is well worth it.

THE WHITE HART HOTEL is a popular old coaching inn which traces its history back at least to the 15th century. It has a comfortable bar and restaurant, as well as an attractive terrace where walkers can order from a selection of menus. ☎ 01256 892900.

The Walk

❶ Turn right out of the Silk Mill car park. After about 250 metres you turn right (opposite a bus shelter) to follow a narrow country lane called The Weir. Cottages on your left precede fields and trees as you approach a former mill on the River Test, where you turn right to follow a hard-surfaced path with the river on your right.

❷ Within a few hundred metres the path turns left, away from the river, and joins a road directly opposite Whitchurch parish church, which is well worth a visit. Cross over and turn right, past the King's Arms pub to the town centre. Here five roads meet, with the White Hart Hotel in view on a left corner. Follow London Street to (or past) the White Hart and then on past the Red House pub to take the second right-hand turning, Town Mill Lane.

❸ Follow the lane to its end

The Test at Whitchurch & Laverstoke ❾

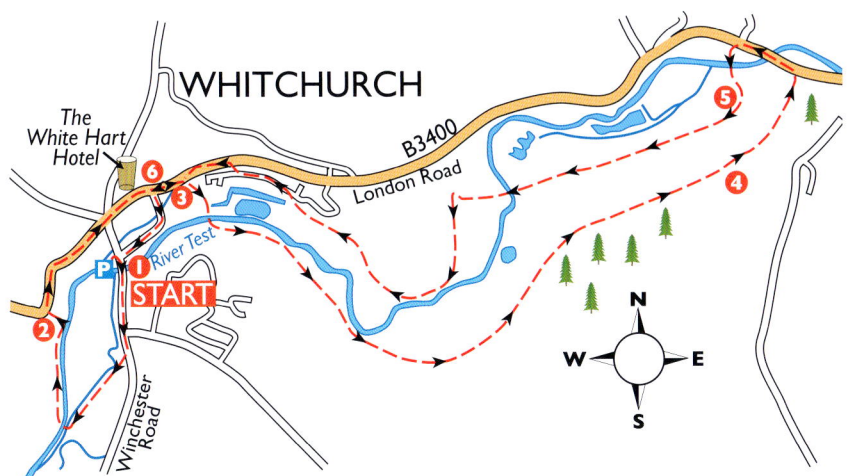

and by Town Mill House cross the Test itself and turn left to follow a path, with trees and the river to your left and arable chalkland to your right. About ½ mile along this well-used public footpath go through a kissing gate on your left. Follow a tributary path, through bushes and then along a winding valley with a woodland slope on your right. Cross a further gate and then, after a distance, head onto another gate. Follow the field edge on the right-hand side. Here, at the tree line, go through a kissing gate and follow the right-hand side of the next field, with woodland rising to your right. The upper Test Valley spreads its scenic treasures to your left as you continue along the woodland edge.

❹ At the end of the field the way drops down and you pass through the hedge onto a sunken track. You cross this and the kissing gate opposite into another wide field of open parkland. Bear slightly left and walk across it to pass to the right of two large successive cedars and head for a metal gate with a kissing gate to its right-hand side. The white circular tower of Freefolk Church is now visible and Laverstoke village is to the right and behind you. The cottages you can see were mostly built to accommodate workers at the paper mill owned by the Portals. This French Huguenot family brought their skills to Britain 300 years ago to escape the persecution then being meted out to Protestants in Louis XIV's France. Now based in larger premises at nearby Overton, the enterprise they founded at Laverstoke has specialised in the making of

Waterside Walks in Hampshire

paper for banknotes, British and foreign. In early days, water-power from the River Test was used for this purpose.

Turn left at the road. At Freefolk, only a few metres farther west in the Whitchurch direction, a terrace of highly photogenic thatched cottages lies back behind gardens on your right. Almost opposite is a lane which leads you left, bridging the Test before passing Freefolk's 13th-century church of St Nicholas.

5 After the church the lane leads right. At a cottage follow the lane left to reach a kissing gate on the right. Pass through it to follow the path across a long meadow, keeping to the higher ground. The river is now down on your right and a line of trees marks the route ahead. The path continues to a kissing gate in the left-hand corner of the meadow. Continue across the next field to a kissing gate just left of a house. Here you join and follow ahead a lane which bridges the Test. A few hundred metres after crossing the river, turn left through a kissing gate. Head straight across the meadow to another kissing gate, and then follow the clear path to a gate. The path develops into a track which fairly soon leads on into a road serving a modern housing development. This eventually brings you out onto the main road where you turn left towards Whitchurch.

6 Turn left at Test Road and follow it over the river, and round to the right to reach Winchester Street, almost opposite Whitchurch Silk Mill and the car park alongside it.

Walk 10
MICHELDEVER & THE DEVER VALLEY
3½ miles (5.5 km)

Start: The Half Moon & Spread Eagle, Winchester Road, Micheldever, SO21 3DG.

Parking: Customers of the Half Moon & Spread Eagle may leave their cars in the large pub car park. Alternatively, park roadside outside the pub. There is also a small car park at the playing field off Duke Street.

OS Map: Explorer 132 Winchester and 144 Basingstoke.
Grid Ref: SU516388.
Terrain: Wooded paths and open fields. Dog friendly.

A lovely village and a crystal-clear chalk stream in the rural heart of Hampshire make a happy combination on this footpath-and-bridleway walk. The parish church of rather unusual design is on the route and is well worth a visit. At Micheldever and elsewhere in Hampshire, there has been a historical reluctance to recognise the Dever as a river,

Waterside Walks in Hampshire

or even to agree on its having a name of any sort. Delving into written records, we find vague references to a North Brook, which also happens to be the name of the part of Micheldever which lies north of the brook in question. People now though acknowledge it as a river, albeit a smallish one at this point, only a mile or so from its source. Pronounce it to rhyme with 'beaver', notwithstanding the fact that the village itself should correctly be pronounced as 'Mitchel-deh-vuh'. Such, so often, are the unexplained incongruities of spoken English!

THE HALF MOON & SPREAD EAGLE is a traditional country pub dating back to 1703. Open every day except Monday and Tuesday, this popular inn serves home cooked food in the cosy restaurant or in the large attractive garden.
☎ 01962 774150.

The Walk

1 Head to the back of the Half Moon & Spread Eagle pub car park and go through the gate and the beer garden, then another gate and across the field to the right-hand corner ahead which leads onto a woodland bridleway track. Turn left and follow it gently downhill. Cross a road onto a continuation bridleway track as it leads you away from the village. This becomes an unfenced farm track as it leads into arable farmland.

2 Halfway across this arable field is a crossing of tracks with a row of trees in view ahead of you, and the end of another line of trees to the right running along a field boundary. Turn right here to follow what is known as 'Coffin Walk', so named from the days before cars when the dead from nearby West and East Stratton were conveyed by handcart to Micheldever for burial. The handcart in question can still be seen in Micheldever church. In 300 metres you enter a wooded field boundary between gently rising ground to your right and to your left a shallow vale within which winds the River Dever, still little more than a narrow stream at this point. The bridleway continues for ½ mile through a wider copse of beech and hazel. At a signed crossing of tracks within this woodland, and with a metal gate just ahead to your right, turn left towards the village of West Stratton and head downhill to cross over the Dever, here close to its source.

3 In around 400 metres you will reach a gate on the left-hand side, if you reach Stratton End

Micheldever & the Dever Valley 10

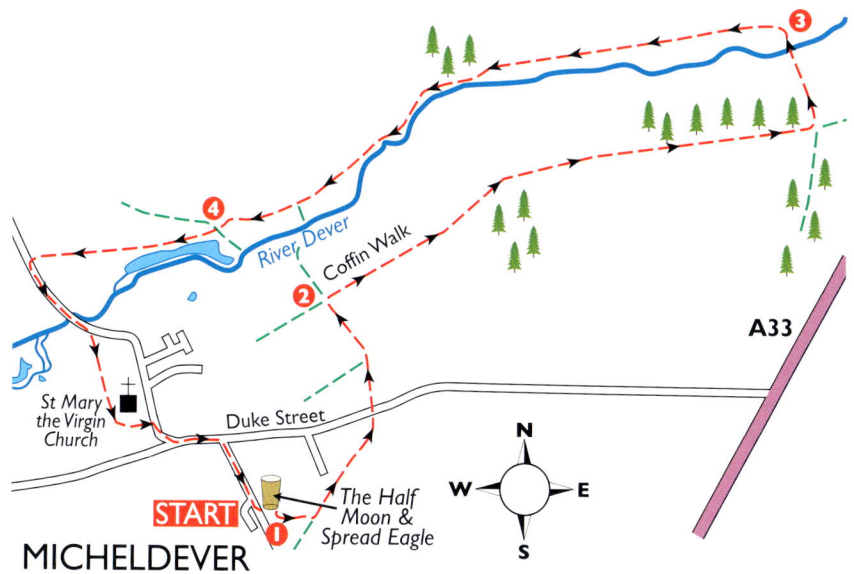

house you have gone too far. Enter a long field and continue straight ahead, keeping the field boundary to your right-hand side and the River Dever to your left. Towards the end of this field the river draws closer to the path as you pass through a second gate. The path curves round to the left here, bounded by a thick

Waterside Walks in Hampshire

The medieval St Mary the Virgin church in Micheldever

hedgerow on your right-hand side and the River Dever on your left, winding its way through a small copse. Continue to a third gate, emerging into an open field with the houses of Northbrook and Micheldever church in the distance. Follow the field boundary straight ahead.

④ Towards the end of this field the Dever, glimpsed through tall conifers, turns into a widened lake. Pass through a wide gap in the fence line, and continue down the slight slope to Northbrook past two large field trees, aiming for the thatched cottage and primitive Methodist Chapel behind. Go through a gate onto a path bounded by garden hedges, emerging soon onto the road at Northbrook. Turn left along the road and after 150 metres or so there is the last of the views of the River Dever on the left-hand side, with a handy bench under a willow tree. Take a footpath on the right-hand side a few metres further on, and up the slight slope to Micheldever Church, St Mary the Virgin, which is well worth a visit and in a beautiful setting. Walk around the church and head downhill to rejoin the road. Cross over onto the pavement and turn right. Follow the road round to the left onto Duke Street, then turn right at the war memorial for the Half Moon & Spread Eagle, or continue straight on for the playing fields car park.

Walk 11
DOGMERSFIELD & THE BASINGSTOKE CANAL
3¼ miles (5 km)

Start: Barley Mow Slipway Car Park, The Hurst, Winchfield, RG27 8DE.

Parking: Walkers using the Barley Mow can leave their cars in the pub car park, but there is also a free car park, Barley Mow Slipway Car Park, beside the canal only metres away.

OS Map: Explorer 144 Basingstoke, Alton & Whitchurch.
Grid Ref: SU778538.

Terrain: Hard surfaced towpath and field paths. Dog friendly.

Step back in time to the 18th-century as you follow this peaceful canal-side walk through a quiet corner of north-east Hampshire. Little has changed since horses first hauled barges along this waterway. The only inland waterway in Hampshire which is navigable today

Waterside Walks in Hampshire

is the Basingstoke Canal, opened in 1796 as a route for the conveyance of heavy merchandise to and from London and the coast via the rivers Wey and Thames. Like so many other canals built around that time, decline soon set in with the arrival of the railway. Leisure use continued for a time, and then for many years the waterway lay derelict and neglected. It suffered what seemed a mortal blow to any hopes of a second revival when the canal tunnel roof at Greywell, north of Odiham, collapsed. In the 1960s, however, a group of enthusiasts launched the Surrey and Hampshire Canal Society. By the early 1990s bridges had been repaired and strengthened, the towpath made good once more and it was again possible for pleasure craft to navigate the waterway. Many have thus rediscovered the charm of this part of northern Hampshire.

THE BARLEY MOW lies in quiet countryside within metres of the canal and is popular with locals and visitors alike. The wooden floors throughout the bar area mean that walkers and well behaved dogs are welcomed. There is also a separate conservatory dining area, a log fire in winter and a patio and garden for fine sunny days. ☎ 01252 617490.

The Walk

❶ Head to the back of the Barley Mow Slipway Car Park to join the Basingstoke Canal Towpath. With Barley Mow Bridge behind you and the canal on your right, follow the hard-surfaced towpath for around 1 mile as it curves right with the canal. Houses in Dogmersfield village can just be glimpsed on your left, the road that serves them at first running closely parallel with the canal and then diverging from it, with fields and woodlands intervening. At one stage the canal cleaves through a cutting, followed by an embankment with the water at a higher level than the bordering land. Pines and rhododendrons on the canal's far side precede a gap through which a wider expanse of water reveals itself – this is 20-acre Tundry Pond, a prime feature of Dogmersfield Park, which you will enter after leaving the towpath at Blacksmith's Bridge, just around the corner from where you now stand.

❷ Cross the bridge and then pass through a gate to join a fenced track which goes right and then left around open fields to skirt the south side of Tundry Pond, a haven for Canada geese and wild ducks. *Coming soon into view on higher ground, and overlooking the park*

Dogmersfield & the Basingstoke Canal 11

from your left, is Dogmersfield House, now a luxury hotel. Built in 1728 on the site of a one-time bishop's palace, it became the seat of the Mildmay family. At the turn of the 18th century, the family had Dogmersfield village moved, lock, stock and barrel, to where it is now, behind the house, so as not to impinge upon their view. A few years earlier, Sir Henry Mildmay had compelled the canal company to divert their intended waterway in a wide loop around Dogmersfield Park as another move to protect his privacy.

Centuries earlier, Henry VI often stayed at Dogmersfield, and it was here that plans were made for the short-lived marriage of Henry VII's

Basingstoke Canal – view over Tundry Pond

Dogmersfield & the Basingstoke Canal

son and heir, Arthur, to Catherine of Aragon who, when widowed, became the first wife of Arthur's brother, Henry VIII.

Continuing our route, where Tundry Pond narrows and is spanned by a bridge, turn left through a gate towards Dogmersfield House along a fenced estate road, then after a very short distance you turn sharp right and along a road. The pond remains on your right. You now make your way across open ground towards Sprat's Hatch Farm and its outbuildings – skirting to the right of some ornate gates.

❸ When you reach the farm precincts, cross through a kissing gate and then follow a bridleway to the left, heading by way of a green lane to Sprat's Hatch Bridge across the canal. From the far side of this you descend to the right to join the towpath once more. Heading north-east now, with the canal on your right, walk into a scene little altered since the early days of the canal. Occasional isolated houses only serve to emphasise the peace of their immediate surroundings. Keep ahead for 1¼ miles passing two further brick bridges spanning the canal before a third one, Barley Mow Bridge, signals the end of your walk through this lovely, unspoilt area.

Walk 12
FROYLE & THE WEY VALLEY
5 miles (7.8 km)

Start: The Hen and Chicken Inn, Upper Froyle, GU34 4JH.

Parking: Park at the Hen and Chicken Inn if visiting (with landlord permission). Alternatively, there is some parking space on the adjacent service road.

OS Map: Explorer 144 Basingstoke. **Grid Ref:** SU756422.

Terrain: Many stiles, some of which are not dog friendly. Uneven field paths and quiet lanes with some relatively steep inclines.

A countryside walk through the beautiful Wey Valley starting in the picturesque village of Froyle. The River Wey, a tributary of the River Thames, was one of the first rivers in England to be made navigable, and you will cross it several times. Catch a

Froyle & the Wey Valley [12]

glimpse of the crystalline waters so characteristic of Hampshire's chalk streams and admire the lush valley through which it winds, taking in views of the county that stretch for miles. This, along with attractive field paths and lovely lanes make for a delightful ramble.

THE HEN AND CHICKEN INN, at one stage, became a gathering place on Sundays for rowdy horse and other livestock dealers, apparently including poultry; hence, perhaps, the name by which the inn has been known ever since. These days the pub is deservedly popular with travellers and locals alike.
☎ 01420 22115.

The Walk

1 Watch out for fast traffic as you cross from the Hen and Chicken onto the grass central reservation of the A31 dual carriageway. Go right for some 200 metres along the reservation and then carefully cross the northbound carriageway into a lane on the other side. Follow the lane over a railway bridge and then in 300 metres across the River Wey, on which is a weir between you and the timber-framed former mill house. At the road junction, turn left beside the former lodge to Mill Court, then walk up the hill. The Court and associated buildings are over the wall on your left with a steep, tree-lined bank on your right. The lane levels out and you soon emerge into the open countryside with fields on either side.

Carry on along this gently undulating road, with its wonderful views down to the river valley below.

2 In 1 mile you reach a T-junction. Turn left and continue downhill for about 100 metres, where you will see a stile through a gap in the hedge on the left. Cross this and turn right, following the hedge now on your right to another stile just past the corner of the field. Go over these stiles and cross the paddock to another stile. From this stile, go down some steps to cross the Alton to Farnham railway line with care. Go up the steps on the other side and follow the short path to another stile into a field. Follow the path with trees on your left to a kissing gate, then proceed across this large field heading towards the buildings seen in the distance. Make for an oak tree by the opposite hedge and, to its right, you can cross a stile onto a minor road.

3 Turn left and cross the River Wey by a small bridge. Climb gently up the road past Froyle Mill, now a private house. Just

57

Waterside Walks in Hampshire

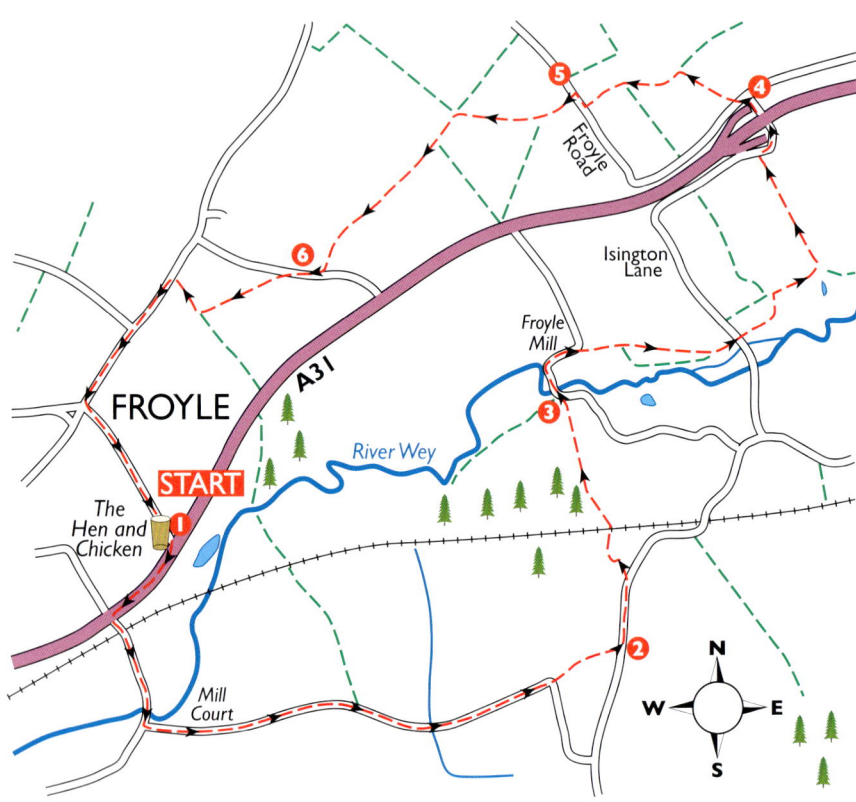

before the brow of the hill and houses come into view, you will see a gate on your right. Cross this into the field and keep the hedge on your right. At the end of the tree line the path goes diagonally right across the field. Follow this to the bottom of the field, where a small lane leads to a minor road (Isington Lane). Cross over to the footpath opposite. *To your right now can be seen another bridge over the Wey and also Isington Mill, with its oast house towers.* Follow the footpath along the fenced drive of a house with trees either side. Just before the house is reached, take a stile on your left which has a fingerpost beside it. This leads across a paddock to two further stiles. After taking the second stile, turn right to follow the tree-lined hedge to the corner of the field. Cross a stile on your right-hand side and then turn left, continuing to follow the fence line with the stream on your right towards the A31, which you can hear in the distance.

Froyle & the Wey Valley 12

4 Cross another stile and keep ahead. When the A31 is reached a gate takes you onto a slip road. Turn right following this slip road to go under the A31. Continue a short distance on this road, passing the other carriageway's slip road. Keep ahead and slightly to the left are white gates and the footpath which runs along the drive to Coldrey House. Walk along the beech-lined drive towards the house until a junction of paths at a hedge. Turn left and continue to walk around the walled garden. Veer left at the Y-junction and continue on a track towards a number of houses.

5 Where the track ends, after the houses, cross the road, taking a stile through the hedge slightly to your right. Follow the hedge, on your left, and cross three more stiles before taking a footpath diagonally right over a field to the opposite hedgerow. Cross the stile and walk ahead under the HT power lines to the opposite fence. If the field is full of crops it is best to walk left along the edge of the field towards the pylon, then after it keep the hedge on your left and walk along the side of the field. At the end of the field the path crosses a small bridge. Cross the bridge, turn left, and follow the drainage ditch on your left. Go

Waterside Walks in Hampshire

through a kissing gate into the next field and continue ahead. At the end of the long, open field you come to a gate and beside it is a kissing gate which you go through onto a minor road, leading to Froyle.

6 Turn right and walk the short distance towards another gated tree-lined drive. Walk along the drive, and at the top of the hill when the trees end and fields open out on the right you will see a gate which you go through heading towards houses and a church. Walk across the field to the road after a stile. At the road turn left, and walk up through the village, past the attractive old village school now converted to a private dwelling. Walk on past Froyle Park, following the road around a left-hand bend which leads you down to the Hen and Chicken.

Walk 13

DROXFORD & THE RIVER MEON

2¼ miles (3.5 km)

Start: The Bakers Arms, High Street, Droxford, SO32 3PA.

Parking: Park at the Bakers Arms if visiting (with landlord permission), or roadside near the village hall and start from point 2.

OS Map: Explorer 119 Meon Valley, Portsmouth, Gosport and Fareham. **Grid Ref:** SU606184.

Terrain: Mostly good footpaths and field paths. A path crosses a natural flood plain, so waterproof boots are advisable. Dog friendly.

Droxford lies on the western slopes of the Meon Valley and this scenic walk shows off some of the area's renowned beauty. The River Meon, less substantial than either the Itchen or the Test, has its source in the South Downs half-a-dozen miles south-west of Petersfield and threads its quiet way to the

Waterside Walks in Hampshire

coast through a succession of villages, of which Droxford is one of the largest and the most ancient. A settlement of some sort almost certainly existed in this location before the Meonwara people, the Jutish tribe that settled in the Meon Valley in the 5th century. They were converted to the Christian faith by St Wilfrid in the 7th century and a cemetery of that period came to light here when the Meon Valley railway was being constructed.

THE BAKERS ARMS is an award-winning, welcoming, dog-friendly pub. There is a cosy wood fire for winter and a sunny patio for the warmer months.
☎ 01489 877533.

The Walk

❶ From the car park at the Bakers Arms, turn left and immediately left again along a narrow passage with a flint wall on your left and a brick one on your right, heading downhill. At the foot of the hill is the driveway of a private house and our footpath forks right, leading to a crossroads of paths and through a kissing gate. *The River Meon, on your left, is a chalk stream fed by springs rather than by rainfall, and it supports a diverse wildlife. Birds such as little egrets are becoming a more common sight, but lucky visitors may see the odd flash of a kingfisher, or if they are very lucky, an otter.* Keep straight ahead. Walk along the right-hand edge of a paddock until you reach the corner of Droxford churchyard; here you turn right through a kissing gate and follow the path ahead keeping the church on your right. Head for a kissing gate in the far corner of the churchyard.

❷ There are several footpaths circling the church, and those using the car park by the village hall can join the walk here. *Droxford's Church of St Mary and All Saints is of 12th-century origin, and visitors can still see the characteristic Norman round-headed doorways on the north and south sides; the inner nave walls and the chancel arch are equally ancient. Izaak Walton who wrote the fisherman's classic* The Compleat Angler, *worshipped here in the 17th century when visiting his daughter, Anne, who had married the rector of Droxford. The river is still well known for its trout fishing.* If starting the walk here, enter the churchyard and pass through a kissing gate in its far right-hand corner. Once through the kissing gate, turn left and follow the tree-lined path which leads you to a footbridge over the River Meon's main channel. Continue to a second footbridge over a minor Meon side-stream.

Droxford & the River Meon 13

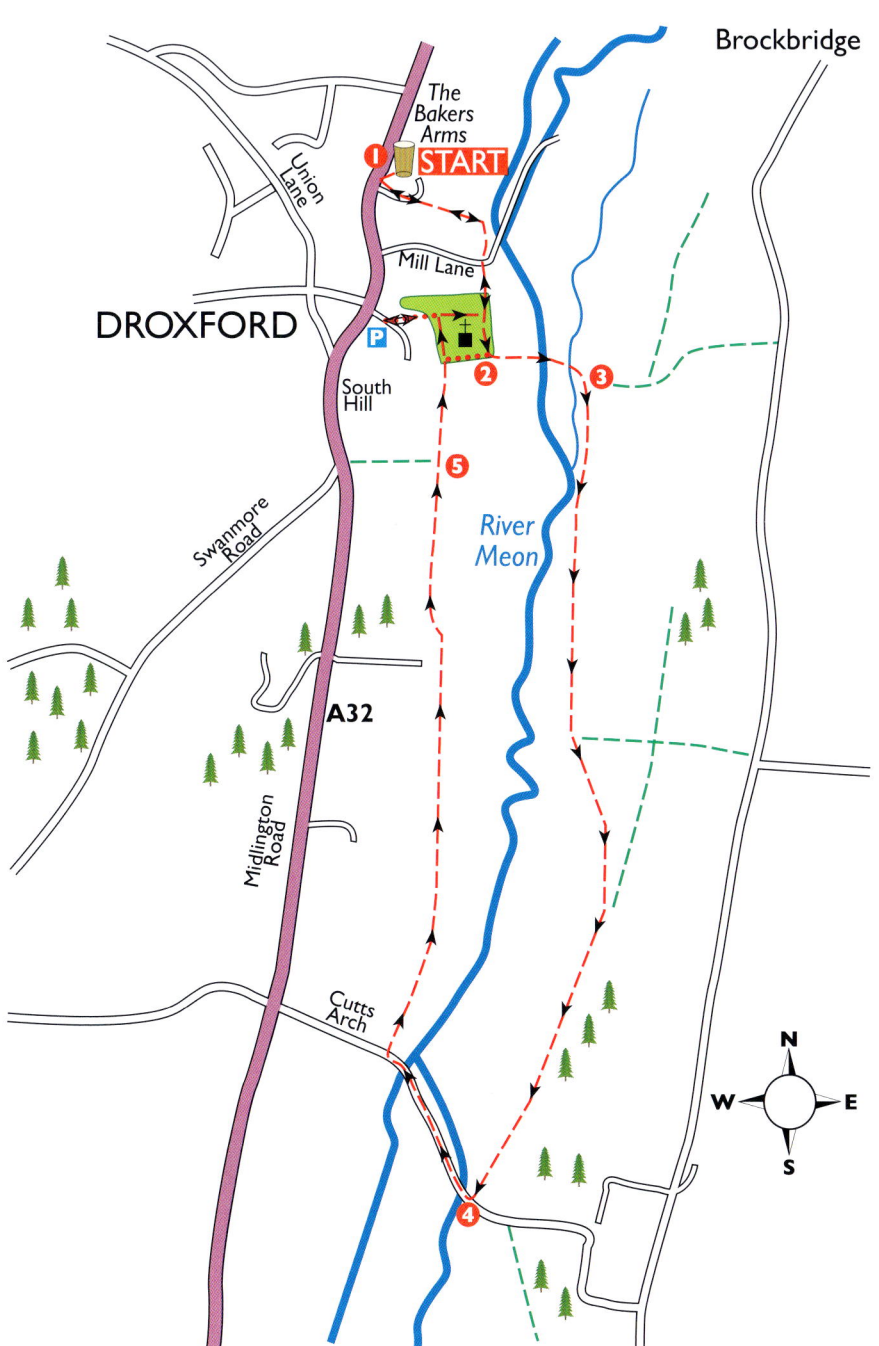

Waterside Walks in Hampshire

3 Beyond this, turn right to go through a kissing gate and follow a section of the Wayfarer's Walk, the long-distance footpath from Emsworth right up to Inkpen Beacon in Berkshire. Pass through the kissing gate at the end of the first field, cross the second field, then keep ahead through the opening into a third field where you make for the higher ground to your left, where there is a clump of tall trees. Once there, cross through the remains of an old stile to another field. Keep ahead, the old track of the railway is now on your left and there are good views of the Meon Valley to the right. You may notice the water in the field below you. It is a natural flood plain and is the reason we make for the higher ground, to avoid it and keep dry feet.

4 At the end of the field, head for the gate, cross over onto the lane and turn right. Soon you cross the main stream of

Droxford & the River Meon 13

the River Meon. At Waterside Cottage on the right-hand side, pass through a kissing gate in the hedge just before the cottage driveway and turn right along a field path, heading back towards Droxford. Follow the hedge-line on the right-hand side, pass through a gap in the hedge, and continue ahead into a long field with views across to the river in places on your right-hand side. Where the field boundary bends sharply away, angle slightly left across the field; the footpath course continues past hedged gardens on the left, then passes a large cream coloured house.

5 At the end of the field cross a kissing gate, and continue straight along the clearly defined footpath. Walk with hedges on both sides and mature trees, and return to the churchyard. Turn left to return to the village hall or keep ahead around the churchyard and retrace your steps back to the Bakers Arms.

Walk 14
Wallington's River Estuary
4¼ miles (6.8 km)

Start: Broadcut Car Park by Wallington Village Hall, PO16 8ST.

Parking: The car park at Wallington Village Hall.

OS Map: Explorer 119 Meon Valley, Portsmouth, Gosport and Fareham. **Grid Ref:** SU583069.

Terrain: No significant gradients, mostly flat gravel path with some roadside pavement. Dog friendly but they will need to be fine with crossing a couple of busy roads.

Surrounded on all sides by busy highways, the little riverside village of Wallington is an oasis of timeless tranquillity. The river which shares the name of the village meets salt water here, after a brief but twisting course around the western shoulder of Ports Down, that isolated chalky eminence

Wallington's River Estuary 14

which overlooks Portsmouth from the north. As you follow the tree-fringed banks of this inlet you will be exploring one of Hampshire's best scenic treasures.

THE COB & PEN is a traditional village pub which is both family and dog friendly. There's a large garden with play area, and it's a popular venue for summer barbecues. ☎ 01329 221624. **CAMS MILL** is a barn-like Fuller's pub overlooking the estuary and viaduct. There is an attractive patio area at the back where you can enjoy the seasonal menu and well-stocked bar. ☎ 01329 287506.

The Walk

❶ Head to the back of the car park and just to the right of the village hall you will see a bridge across the River Wallington. Cross the bridge and turn right. Walk along Wallington Shore Road, passing the Cob and Pen on your left. In ¼ mile you will reach a large roundabout. Keep to the left-hand side of it, passing the Roundabout Hotel and going under the flyover and the Fareham-Portsmouth railway. Reaching the turn-off for Portchester and Cosham by the Delmé Arms pub, cross carefully over the main road to the right-hand side of Cams Mill pub on the opposite side. Here you

Waterside Walks in Hampshire

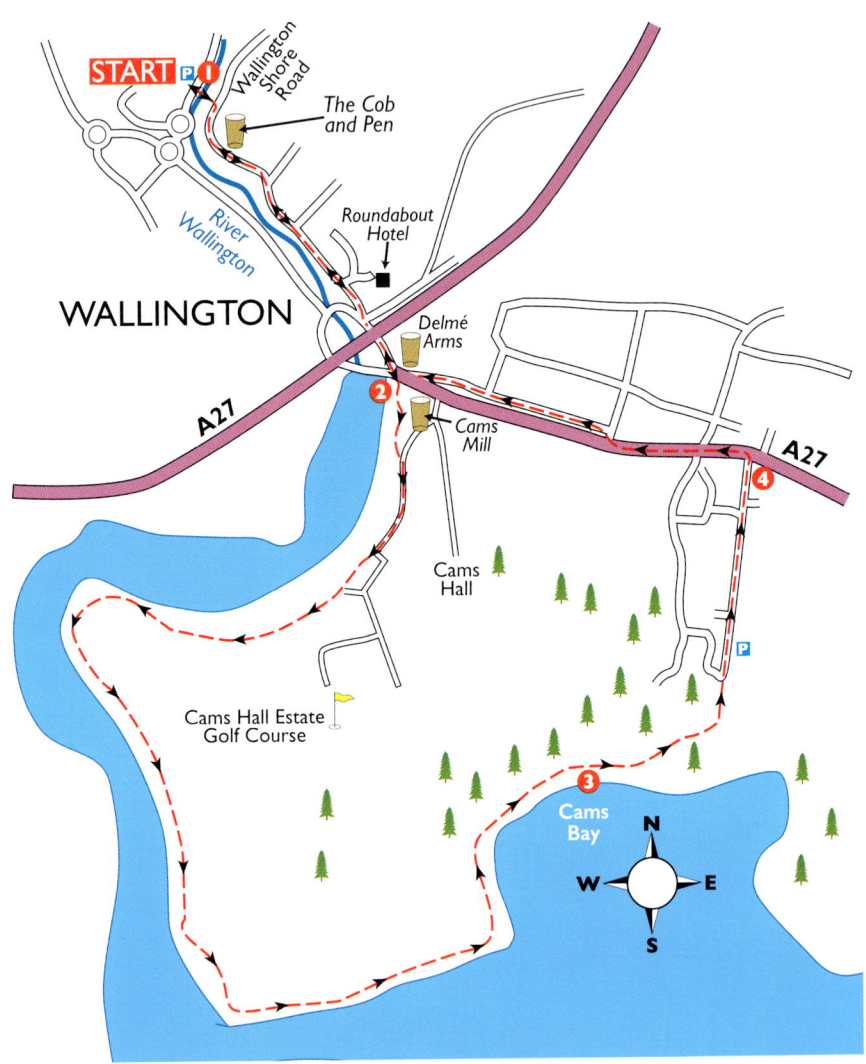

will see a footpath that takes you around the back and along the edge of the (now tidal) river and estuary. There is a good view across to Fareham, where trains rumble over Wallington Viaduct, built in 1848.

❷ Keep on this gravel path through the trees with the water on your right. Most of the surrounding former farmland is now a golf course, whose grassy acres spread out to your left as you keep to the track closest to the estuary edge. As

Wallington's River Estuary 14

the widening estuary wriggles around Cams Hall Estate golf course the scene becomes increasingly peaceful and rural.

3 After nearly two miles, the path comes to Cams Bay and the end of the golf course. Go through the gate and overhead you'll see pylon lines with the main track continuing ahead. However, we turn diagonally left along a grassy track which follows the pylon lines. After a short distance there is another gate and the path meets a track. Turn left and keep ahead onto the residential street, Birdwood Grove, which leads up to the main A27 road.

4 Turn left along this road. At the lights, cross over and continue along the other side of the A27. You soon enter the service road running parallel to the main road. Continue along here (Cams Hill), passing a row of 19th-century cottages. Head on past the Delmé Arms, retracing your steps to the Cob and Pen. Follow the road round to the right past the pub until you reach the bridge on your left. Cross over to return to the car park.

Fareham

Walk 15
Titchfield & the Lower Meon Valley

5¼ miles (8.5 km)

Start: Titchfield Canal Car Park, Bridge Street, Titchfield, PO14 4EA.

Parking: There is a small free car park alongside Bridge Street, where this crosses the old canal, but this often becomes full at busy times. A larger car park off Southampton Hill can be used for a maximum stay of 3 hours. Alternative limited free parking space may be found along the High Street or West Street.

OS Map: Explorer 119 Meon Valley, Portsmouth, Gosport and Fareham.
Grid Ref: SU541054.

Terrain: Canal-side paths and good footpaths with a short stretch along a fairly busy road. Dog friendly.

Titchfield & the Lower Meon Valley 15

Titchfield is one of Hampshire's unspoiled architectural gems. A haven of tranquillity and a peaceful backwater tucked away amid rural greenery yet so close to the urban development that now almost unites Southampton and Portsmouth. Here lovely Georgian cottages flank ancient streets and, fittingly, Titchfield's church of St Peter is one of the oldest in the county, with a history dating back to the 8th century. The route starts by the canal, along a path that takes us down to the Solent shore. From there a clifftop walk will complete an exceptional and memorable outing.

There are several pubs and cafés in the centre of Titchfield. Alternatively, a short drive away is **THE TITCHFIELD MILL**, part of the Vintage Inns chain with a classic country pub menu and attractive garden ☎ 01329 840931, or Greene King's **FISHERMANS REST** a little further along the road opposite Titchfield Abbey ☎ 01329 845065.

The Walk

❶ Starting from the canal-side car park off Bridge Street, turn left away from the main road to follow a well-defined path through a metal gate and then a kissing gate. Continue along this path with the canal to your right-hand side for around 2 miles. *The canal's artificial origin is emphasised by the straight course it follows, flanked on one side by your footpath, and by trees on the other side. The watermeadows of Titchfield Haven lie to your left, overlooked by a timbered slope which screens from view much of the residential housing of Stubbington on that side of the Meon Valley.*

❷ On passing through another gate, the footpath exits onto Meon Road where this spans the canal on a sharp bend. *The low bridge is a restored version of the sea-lock, through which the barge traffic had to pass to enter the freshwater canal to reach Titchfield.* Follow the wooded path running adjacent to the road on the left-hand side, which continues south beside Titchfield Haven National Nature Reserve, where you'll find many species of waterbird. When you reach the chalets near the shoreline turn right passing through the opening in the fence to cross Meon Shore road to a gate and a footpath with beach chalets on both sides.

❸ Walk right between the chalets, then turn left towards the beach (which you can access at this point). Turn immediately right to follow the coastal path, the Solent Way, which goes along the top of a gravelly cliff

Waterside Walks in Hampshire

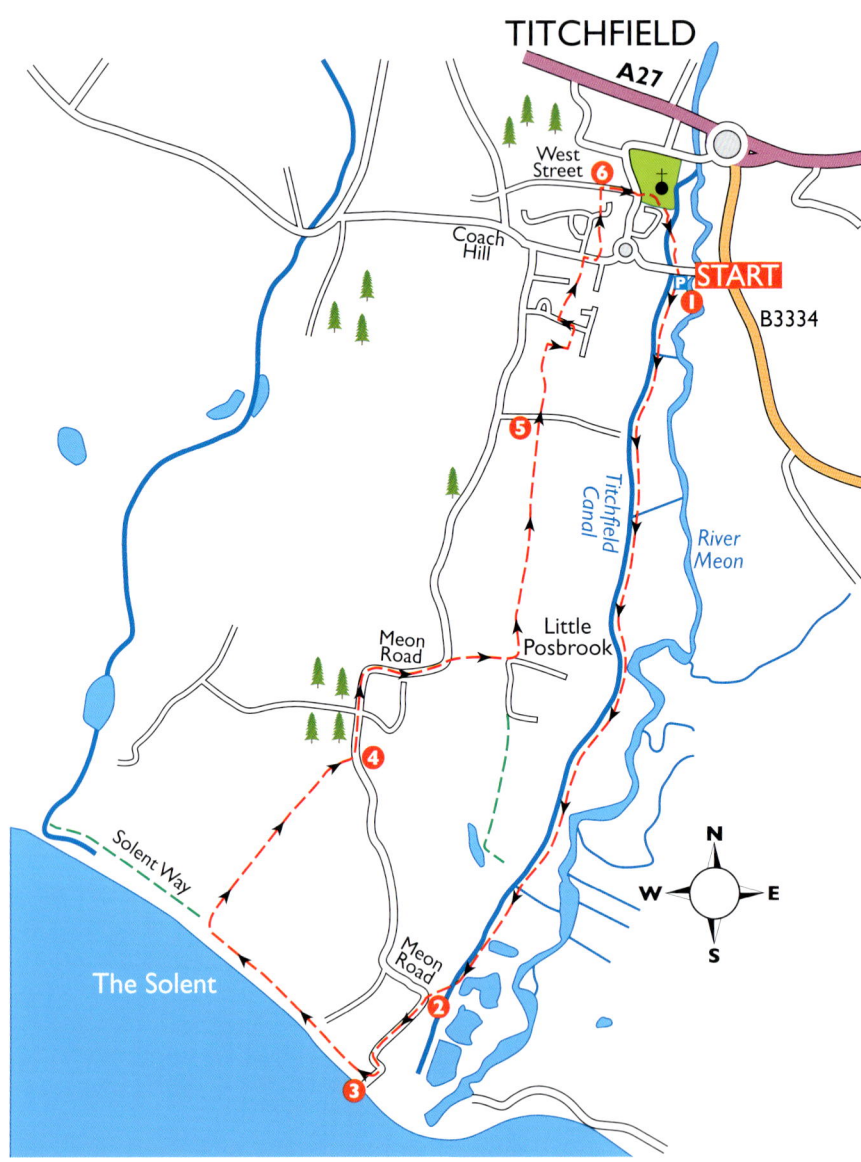

with the sea on your left. Bushes sheltering the path along much of its length are punctuated by gaps through which you can see right across the Solent to Fawley and Calshot on the New Forest coastline, and to the Isle of Wight. Within ½ mile at the end of a very large field, turn right down a pathway between

Titchfield & the Lower Meon Valley 15

the fields and away from the coast. At the end of the large fields, go through a kissing gate, turn left and then right over a small wooden bridge and into Thatchers Coppice. Here your path winds through oaks and hazels before emerging through a car park onto Meon Road.

4 Turn left, taking care on this sometimes fast and busy road, keep into the verges as the road soon bends to the right. Where it turns sharply left continue straight ahead along a farm road which doubles as a footpath. Follow this with a large hedge on one side and fields to the right. Ignoring the first adjoining farm track on your left, continue to where two farm tracks cross, where you turn left. Continue along this farm lane past a farm on the right-hand side, and at a second property on the right as the farm track bends to the right continue straight on along a grassy footpath between large fields, with views of the Meon Valley dipping beyond.

5 At the end of the large field, cross straight over the approach road to Great Posbrook Farm via a kissing gate and stile, emerging

Waterside Walks in Hampshire

into a meadow. Keep straight on heading towards a children's play area and exit the field by a row of garages at the back of Bellfield housing estate. Bear right from the garages along a concrete path and turn left into Ransome Close, then left again along Hewett Road, and right along Lower Bellfield. You will then come to Coach Hill, which you follow right for a few metres, then take a left along a tarmacked footpath. This soon crosses another road and is flanked by a very old wall partly constructed of herringbone brickwork before emerging onto West Street.

6 Old-world Titchfield spreads before you as you turn right and continue downhill to the village square. *The steepled church beckons at the end of narrow Church Street, straight ahead – spare time if you can for at least a brief visit. To the right of the chancel, in an exhibition area is the massive Wriothesley Memorial, to the family who owned Titchfield after the abbey was closed down.* A path to the right of the church leads to a footbridge across the canal, where you turn right, with the canal once again on your right, to head back to Bridge Street and the car park.

Vicky Fletcher

Walk 16
BURSLEDON & THE HAMBLE ESTUARY
4¾ miles (7.5 km)

Start: Bursledon Railway Station, Station Road, Bursledon, SO31 8AA.

Parking: Bursledon Railway Station Car Park.

OS Map: Explorer 119 Meon Valley, Portsmouth, Gosport and Fareham. **Grid Ref:** SU489095.

Terrain: Some uneven paths that can get very muddy. A few stiles but each has a gap for smaller dogs to get through.

This walk explores the quieter reaches of this yacht-thronged estuary. The well-wooded Manor Farm Country Park and a farm with a café halfway along the route also add to the pleasure of the walk.

While the freshwater Hamble, above Botley, is one of Hampshire's shorter rivers, the tidal estuary into which it flows is the longest in the county. Between Bursledon and Southampton Water, the

Waterside Walks in Hampshire

Hamble Estuary is also one of the busiest in Britain, with more yachts and other pleasure craft per square kilometre of water than almost any other seaway in the country.

THE JOLLY SAILOR is the perfect spot to get views across the water and watch the comings and goings of boats on the busy river. The pub is right next to the water and even has its own pontoon, so is also accessible by boat depending on the tide. Once Church property and the home of a local clergyman, this was originally a cottage which had no links with the licensed trade until, around 100 years ago, it was sold to a Southampton brewer. Old beams, a flagstone floor and bull's-eye window panes looking out onto the river all help preserve an old-world atmosphere. For sunny days there are picnic tables right by the river. ☎ 02380 405557.

The Walk

To get to the Jolly Sailor before or after the walk, with the station and railway on your left-hand side, walk through the car park and follow a hard surfaced footpath up the wooded bank. When you join a road at the top, turn left. You can either follow the road to the top entrance of the pub enjoying views across the Hamble, or turn left down to the river bank. This route passes the entrance to the historic Elephant Boatyard, commemorating Nelson's flagship at the

Bursledon & the Hamble Estuary 16

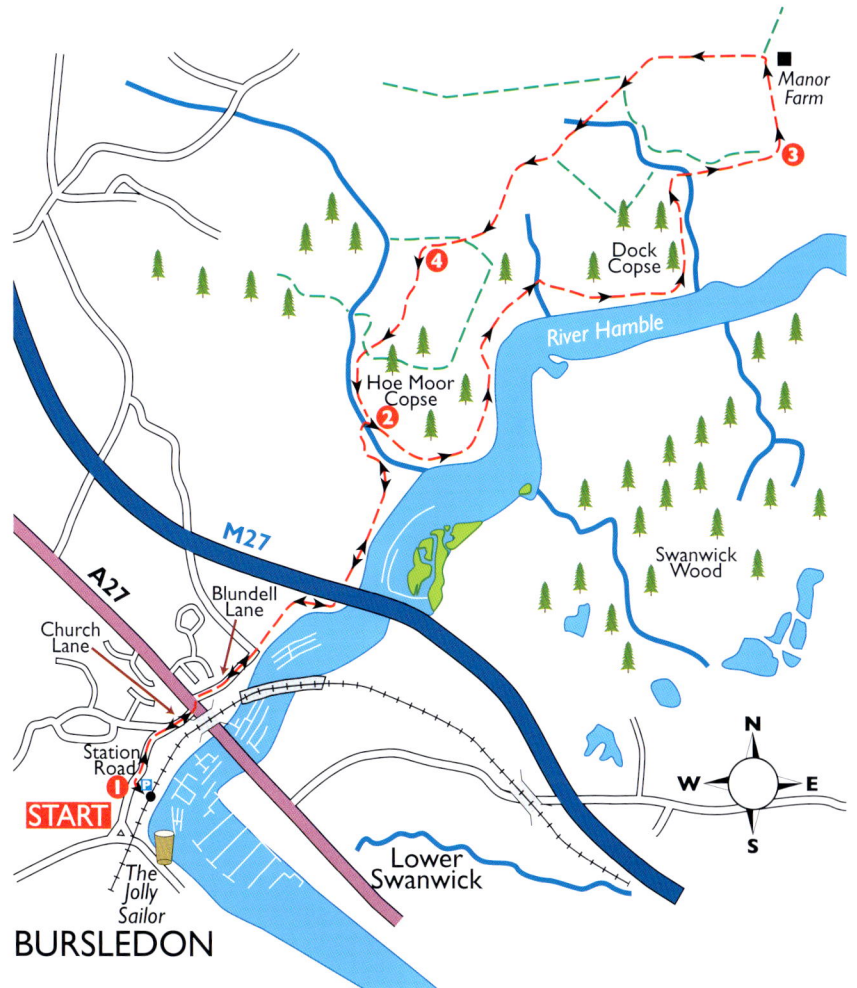

Battle of Copenhagen, HMS *Elephant*; at the river edge follow the public footpath to the right towards the pub. On your return to the station you can follow the footpath back down, or walk down Station Road which runs parallel to the path, closed to motorised traffic.

❶ Walk along Station Road and then turn right into Church Lane to carefully cross the busy A27 by the railway bridge. Blundell Lane now leads straight on. Where the road bends left, continue ahead on a public footpath through Foulkes and Sons Riverside Boatyard and continue along a

Waterside Walks in Hampshire

lane which bends to the right before passing under the M27. Just short of Brixedone Farm, cross a stile on your right into a riverside meadow. Follow the path through the meadow. On reaching a tidal creek bear left inland for 100 metres or so, then right crossing a stile and footbridge over the creek into Manor Farm Country Park. *From here you will be following the Strawberry Trail, so called because these soft fruits have been harvested in the Hamble Valley for over 150 years giving it the title of the 'Strawberry Coast'. The boom began in the late 1860s. Before fridges, the railways played an important part in delivering this eagerly awaited seasonal fruit as quickly as possible to towns and cities across the country.*

❷ Turn right to follow a hard-surfaced path firstly along the creek and then bending left, once again parallel with the River Hamble estuary, viewed through a screen of trees on your

Bursledon & the Hamble Estuary 16

right. The path soon leads to a pontoon which is located close to the sunken wreck of what is thought to have been Henry V's great warship *Grace Dieu*, struck by lightning and destroyed by fire in 1439. A waterside path leads you on from here to rejoin the main path, from which another subsidiary path soon diverges right down steps to the river bank again. From this point on keep as close to the river as paths permit, with a fence on your right-hand side, until you reach a crossing of paths where the fence and its accompanying path bend sharply right, downhill towards the river. Follow this path over a bridge keeping to the path closest to the water as it winds through the trees. The path is uneven and often muddy so take care. Follow the path round to the left with the creek to your right. At the T-junction of paths turn right heading downhill and then up wide log steps the other side. Keep ahead emerging from the trees where you join a wide track on your left. Turn right along the track with a large field to your left.

❸ At the path junction turn left towards Manor Farm itself, with a visitor centre, car park and café. To continue the walk turn left by the car park to follow a gravel path directly alongside a hedged lane which you might not recognise as part of a Roman road. Where the gravelled way presently turns left, continue ahead, with the hedged lane still beside you. Beyond the lane is a small wood where charcoal-burning kilns are present.

❹ Enter woodland, following a hard path leading to a picnic area and children's play area. Ignore side turnings and continue ahead, through the wood to a path-junction by the creek at its far end. Here you turn right and then left across the footbridge at the head of the tidal creek to rejoin your outward route, which you follow back to Bursledon.

Walk 17
Calshot & Southampton Water
4¼ miles (6.8 km)

Start: The Jolly Sailor, Ashlett Road, SO45 1DT.

Parking: Walkers using the Jolly Sailor can leave their cars in the pub car park opposite. There is also a small free car parking area at Ashlett Creek nearby. The area around the Mill is private parking for the club only.

OS Map: Explorer OL22 New Forest. **Grid Ref:** SU467032.

Terrain: Good hard shoreline paths. Two stiles but both have gaps for smaller dogs.

An old tide-mill and a quiet coast where seabirds congregate survive along this stretch of Southampton Water's western shoreline, made accessible by a footpath many walkers have overlooked. Here there is history, great views, salt water and bracing sea air to invigorate you.

80

Calshot & Southampton Water 17

Calshot is one of the coastal locations where Henry VIII had a castle built to protect his realm against invasion after his rift with the Roman Catholics. However, throughout much of the 20th century it had a defensive role of another kind through its links with aviation - the Royal Flying Corps, the Royal Naval Air Service and the Royal Air Force all having been involved at different stages. Calshot's more recent function has been to serve as a centre for ground and water-based sporting activities.

THE JOLLY SAILOR is a pub with as maritime a flavour throughout as one could wish for in such a setting, and yachting folk whose craft come into the creek at high tide are regulars. There's outside seating with great views for sunny days, and an open fire inside for winter walkers.
☎ 02380 891305.

The Walk

1 With Ashlett Creek and the tide-mill on your left, walk to the end of the car park area where, directly beyond a pedestrian access gate, you turn left to follow a shore-edge footpath. This skirts left of the sailing club premises, with tidal saltmarsh and Southampton Water itself on your left-hand side. You pass through a kissing gate after the sailing club and continue to follow the shoreline. The path soon curves right across grass to join a hard-surfaced footpath flanked by

Waterside Walks in Hampshire

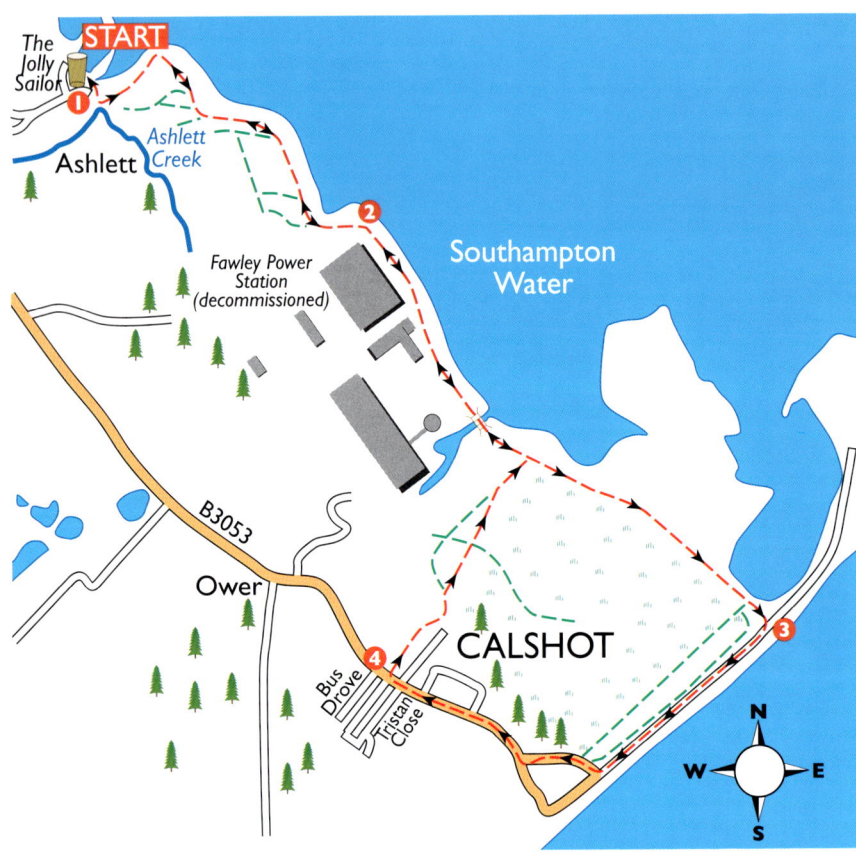

bushes. Follow the path to your left, keeping as close to Southampton Water as you can with either a wide expanse of saltmarsh or tidal creeks directly to your left, depending on the state of the tide.

❷ In ¼ mile your path skirts left of the decommissioned Fawley Power Station, follow the fence around it. Cross an inlet water channel by a bridge with a gate at each end. Continue ahead to Calshot, with a firm path underfoot all the way and sea or saltmarsh still alongside you.

❸ At Calshot, follow the shore road to your right, with the shingly shore to your left – a popular venue on warm summer days. You can walk along the grass at the edge of the road, along a shingle path in front of the beach huts, or along the beach itself depending on the conditions. Follow the direction of the road where it bends to the right, following the marked

Calshot & Southampton Water 17

Ashlett Mill

footway on the side of the car park, heading inland through the village. If you feel in need of refreshment, keep going straight at the first right turn as there is a café a couple of hundred metres further on. Follow the road to the right into the village, where there is a grassy area at the side of the road.

4 At the end of the village, when you pass Tristan Close on the left and before you reach Bus Drove, a footpath sign points your way over a stile to the right along a shallow vale bordered by bushes. After another stile and bridging a small stream, the official public footpath turns left, and then right following the former power station fence, however there is another path to the right which takes you directly to the corner where you turn left. Then follow the shoreline path to the left and back along the edge of Southampton Water. Here you rejoin your original path, which you follow back to Ashlett. There are numerous tracks to the left so avoid these and keep the power station chimney behind you. As you approach Ashlett, you can keep to the hard path if you want to head straight back to your car.

Walk 18
BUCKLER'S HARD & THE BEAULIEU RIVER
4½ miles (7.2 km)

> **Start:** Beaulieu Car Park, Palace Lane, SO42 7PJ.
> **Parking:** There is a pay and display public car park (with toilets) in Beaulieu, behind Beaulieu Garage on Palace Lane (B3054).
> **OS Map:** Explorer OL22 New Forest. **Grid Ref:** SU386021.
> **Terrain:** Mostly flat gravelled tracks or riverside paths. Dog friendly.

Scenic charm of a very high order extends all the way from the beautiful village of Beaulieu to the 18th-century time-warp of Buckler's Hard along this field-and-woodland walk beside the winding estuary. Pastures, trees and tidal water merge their individual charms to provide a potent mixture of scenic delights throughout the route. Beaulieu itself has an extra special magic. Ever since King John made a gift of the manor to the Cistercian monks way back in the 13th century, it has very much been a place apart from the outside world. Today, of course, it is best known as the home of the

Buckler's Hard & the Beaulieu River **18**

National Motor Museum, but people still flock to Beaulieu to enjoy its old-world beauty and the peace of its surroundings between the New Forest and the sea.

THE MONTAGU ARMS HOTEL has been Beaulieu's village inn for well over 200 years. Today a luxury hotel, it embodies a pub, Monty's Inn, ideally located to serve refreshment before and after your walk. ☎ 01590 612324. Try **STEFF'S KITCHEN** next to the garden centre in Beaulieu for lighter options. ☎ 01590 612307. At the **MASTER BUILDER'S HOUSE HOTEL** in Buckler's Hard, the Yachtsman's Bar is open all day, and in good weather you can sit out in front of the pub to enjoy food and drink before walking back to Beaulieu. ☎ 01590 616253.

The Walk

❶ Leave Beaulieu Car Park by the pedestrian exit to the High Street. Cross the High Street to find the waymarked 'footpath to Buckler's Hard 2 miles' opposite. The gravel path leads to a pedestrian gate beyond which you follow the path to the left of a playing-field to another gate. Here you turn right and follow the Solent Way (signposted in places), which is a gravel road through the gate.

❷ The gravelled way leads on between fenced pastures. The Beaulieu River estuary loops between farmland and trees to your left as you carry straight on along a fenced track, soon passing through a finger of woodland bordering a tidal creek. Here you enter North Solent Nature Reserve and continue along a field-edge to Bailey's Hard, where you pass on your left a cottage and a vehicle barrier. The chimney on your left is part of what used to be the brickworks for Beaulieu Manor.

❸ Here you join and follow for a few metres a gravel approach-road. Soon after a right-hand bend, turn left, past another vehicle barrier and along a hard track into a wood called Keeping Copse. Just ahead you will pass on your left a woodland track marked 'private', about 100

Waterside Walks in Hampshire

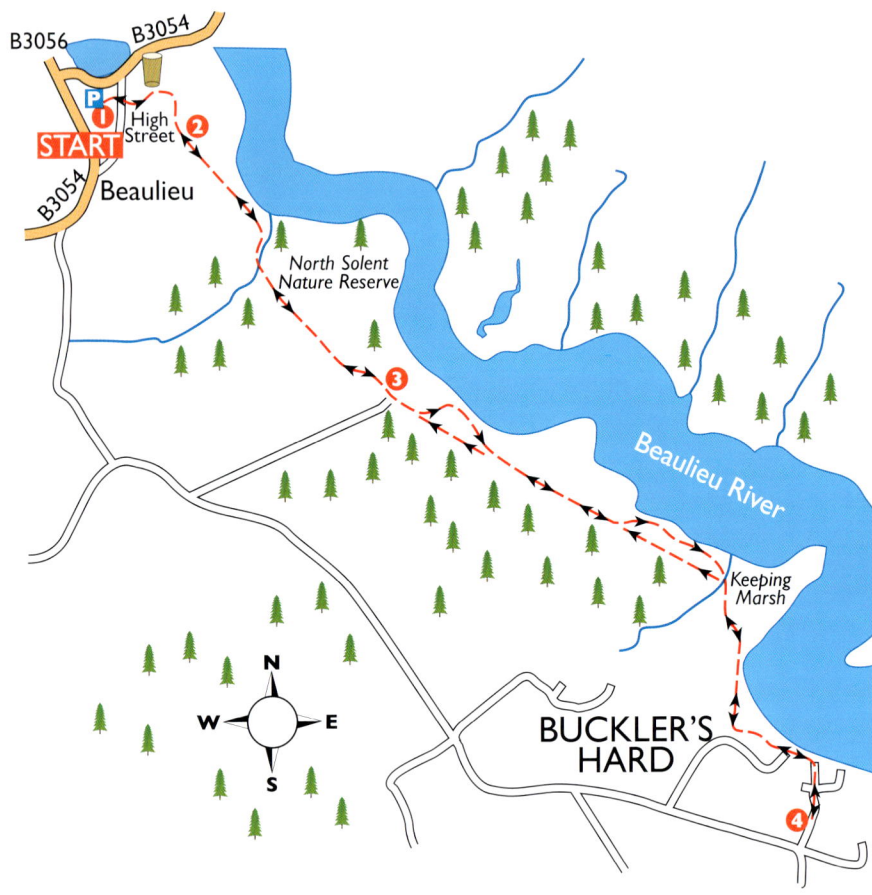

metres beyond which you turn left through a gate to follow a well-used path towards the river (marked Riverside Diversion Western Loop). Sections of this path have boardwalk which makes for easy going even in wet conditions. This loop will take you back to the main track which you follow for a further 500 metres before taking another left-hand gate for the slightly longer Eastern Loop.

Again you will arrive back at the main track which you continue to follow. On the left you can take a 50 metre diversion to the birdwatching hide on Keeping Marsh. Eventually the track skirts Buckler's Hard Yacht Harbour. Do not follow the bicycle route to your right, but cross the approach road and go slightly left to follow the path signposted to Buckler's Hard. Keep ahead

Buckler's Hard & the Beaulieu River ⓲

past the Duke's Bath House to reach Buckler's Hard itself.

❹ The village street, with its wide grass borders and terraced 18th-century dwellings, rises quite steeply from the river, with the pub and the chapel on your right, and the maritime museum at the top, on your left. *The museum displays numerous relics of the times when the village would have been a hive of industry building ships with which England defended itself against Napoleon. The Master Builder's hotel contains the very room where master builder Henry Adams worked. At the bottom of the hill on the right is the Shipwright School workshop, a reproduction building built using traditional tools and techniques. At peak holiday times you can explore still more of the Beaulieu River estuary by taking advantage of one of the boat trips which then operate between Buckler's Hard and the point where the river joins the Solent.* Directions for the return walk are straightforward. Head back down the main street, turn left and follow the river past the Duke's Bath House and across the entrance to Buckler's Hard Yacht Harbour to the Keeping Copse where, instead of following the riverside path for a second time, you can keep to the direct main track. This wide gravel track is almost straight to Bailey Hard where you continue ahead to follow your outward route in reverse. When you pass the second field gate across the track, turn left and follow the path round the playing field back to Beaulieu.

Walk 19
PENNINGTON & THE SOLENT SHORE
3 miles (4.7 km)

Start: The Chequers Inn, Ridgeway Lane, SO41 8AH.

Parking: Walkers using the Chequers may leave their cars in the pub car park. Alternatively, there is some roadside parking a little further along the road.

OS Map: Explorer OL22 New Forest. **Grid Ref:** SZ321935.

Terrain: Mostly hard-surfaced paths and quiet lanes. Dog friendly.

Where salt was once produced from evaporated sea water, there is now a wilderness paradise for birds, and for walkers who enjoy sea breezes and wide open spaces down by the shore.

The Solent sea-wall path on this route provides all of these. The old `salterns' south of Pennington, just a little way west of Lymington, were once the enclosures where sea water

Pennington & the Solent Shore

was evaporated to a point at which the resultant brine could be boiled away, leaving just the salt. This became uneconomic when salt mines in Cheshire were exploited as Britain's main source of the product and the salterns fell into disuse after 1865.

THE CHEQUERS INN is an attractive, creeper-covered building set back a little from a quiet, tree-bordered byway at Lower Woodside, midway between Pennington and the coast. This 16th-century inn was ideally located to cater for thirsty salt workers and was where outgoing salt was checked for tax purposes. Today, it welcomes walkers, families and dogs with a cosy warm stove for winter days and a walled garden for summer. They serve a seasonal menu, as well as bar snacks and barbeques. It is worth booking in advance to guarantee a table. ☎ 01590 673415.

The Walk

1 With your back to the Chequers Inn, turn right along Ridgeway Lane as it becomes Lower Woodside, a quiet, tree-lined lane which passes it. Leave Chequers Green on your right and follow the lane for ½ mile round two right-hand bends until you reach a blind end by some fairly isolated cottages. A hard-surfaced, tree-shaded path continues to the right, skirting left of a small lake where swans are often present.

2 The path leads to Lower Pennington Lane, turn left and

Tim Kermode

Waterside Walks in Hampshire

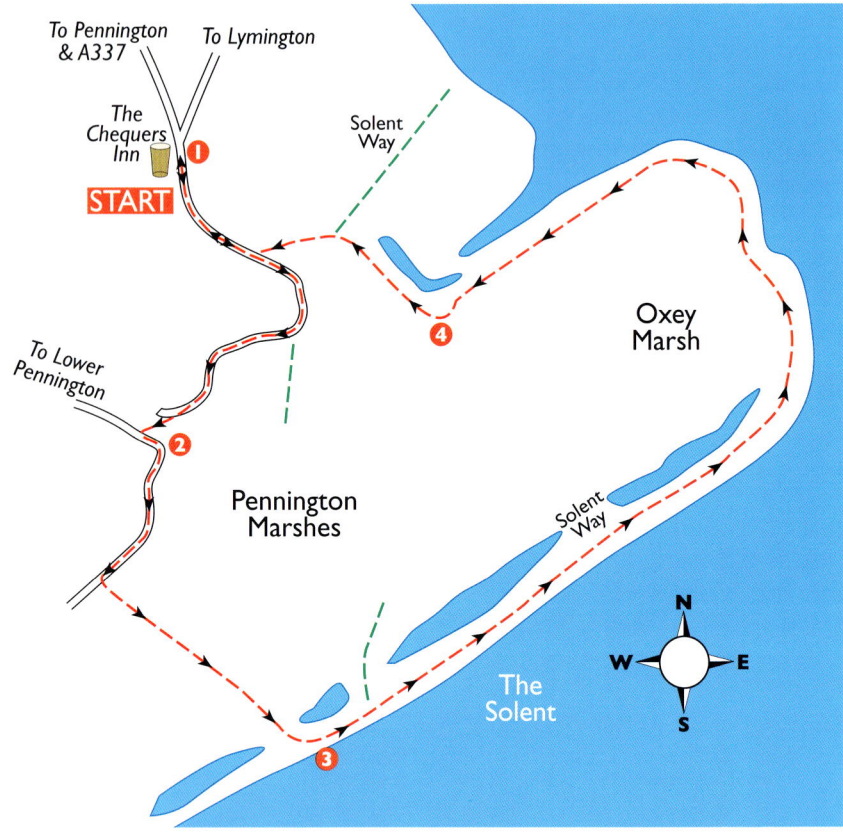

as you follow this it soon bends right, with the level expanse of Pennington Marshes extending to your left. You then approach another blind road end with a small car park. Here turn sharp left to follow a straight gravel track across the marshes. Part of this stretch can become flooded, so if this is the case head for the higher parallel track which will also take you to the Solent sea wall. *To your right, behind the white lighthouse on the end of Hurst Spit you can see the Needles, the nearest town with the distinctive church is Yarmouth and you may notice the ferries arriving from Lymington. Further left you can see the entrance to Cowes. Beyond sheltered water and spreading saltmarsh to your rear stretches Hurst Spit, a shingle spit at the end of which is Hurst Castle, built by Henry VIII as one of a chain of coastal fortresses. Charles I was imprisoned here before being taken to London and his execution. It was extended during the Napoleonic Wars and*

Pennington & the Solent Shore 19

Salt Boiling House

in the 19th century, and during the Second World War coastal gun batteries and searchlights were added. It remains as an enduring reminder of measures taken over the centuries to guard this country against foreign foes. To your left extends that wilderness mosaic of land and water where the salterns used to be and where wetland birds now reign supreme.

3 Raised high enough to protect the town and the freshwater marsh from tidal inundation, the sea wall is topped by a gravel path which you follow to the left, pausing whenever you feel inclined to cast your eye across the sea to the Isle of Wight. As it follows bends in the sea wall, turning to the left your path encompasses Oxey Marsh before turning left again, with a creek known as Moses Dock, alongside it and the Solent proper now behind you. The creek narrows as you approach a substantial sluice gate, which is crossed in its turn by a path. Disregard this and keep straight on, down some steps with a channel of water still to your right.

4 Turn right through a gate and continue to follow the creek. Across the creek you will notice two old brick buildings, these are the only remains of the Salt Boiling Houses that once dominated this area. At the end of the creek do not cross the V-shaped stile, but turn left and follow the tree-lined path for a short distance before turning right onto the lane you took south from the Chequers Inn at Lower Woodside, and which you now follow in reverse.

Walk 20
Ringwood & the Avon Valley Path
4¾ miles (7.6 km)

Start: Furlong Car Park, Stallard's Lane, Ringwood, BH24 1HF.

Parking: The walk starts from Ringwood's large central car park which is clearly signposted. The long stay car park is to the right of the mini roundabout.

OS Map: Explorer OL22 New Forest. **Grid Ref:** SU147054.

Terrain: Field paths, water meadows, farm tracks and some road walking but all with pavement or along quiet lanes. Parts of the route can be extremely wet and boggy even on dry days so tall waterproof boots would be advisable. A few stiles but all with gaps big enough for dogs to pass through.

Hampshire's mightiest river, the River Avon, loops its leisurely way between lush pastures where wild flowers flourish in their multitudes each spring. This walk along water meadow paths and quiet lanes to the south of the ancient town

Ringwood & the Avon Valley Path

of Ringwood provides a close encounter with a chalk stream fuller-bodied than either the Itchen or the Test, the so-called Hampshire Avon, which rises in Wiltshire and ends in Dorset, collecting several other fairly substantial rivers on the way. It also includes a stretch of the Avon Valley Path, the long-distance route between Salisbury and Christchurch. This passes through Ringwood town centre, where you join it at the start of the walk.

THE ORIGINAL WHITE HART in the High Street is so old that efforts to ascertain its actual age have so far proved unsuccessful, but it seems there may have been a hostelry on the same site in the 12th century. With its ancient beams, low ceilings and two inglenook fireplaces, this is a traditional pub in almost every aspect. There is also a cobbled courtyard where visitors can relax in the fine weather, as well as a cosy bar area and restaurant for winter walkers. ☎ 01425 472702. Alternatively, there are also a number of cafés and restaurants on the High Street.

The Walk

1 With the tower of Ringwood's parish church looming a short distance to your right, follow the road past the short stay car park towards the town centre, then turn right along narrow Meeting House Lane. Keep right as you

Tim Kermode

Waterside Walks in Hampshire

enter Ringwood High Street, and the Market Place where The Original White Hart, on your right, is just one of many period buildings. Carry on past the old Market Place, faced on your right by the 19th-century church of St Peter and St Paul. *This replaced a church which dated in part from the 13th century.* Now continue along West Street, before bridging an arm of the River Avon, passing a lovely old thatched and timber-framed cottage which is now a restaurant.

2 Directly after crossing the river, turn left along a road which leads you through a residential caravan park. Walk straight through the caravan park to a kissing gate and you enter a meadow and fenced